healing the heart

healing the heart

*Opening and
Healing the Heart
with Crystals and Gemstones*

Daya Sarai Chocron

SAMUEL WEISER, INC.
York Beach, Maine

First published in English in 1989 by
Samuel Weiser, Inc.
Box 612
York Beach, Maine 03910

Second printing, 1990

Library of Congress Cataloging in Publication Data

Chocron, Daya Sarai.
    Healing the heart.

    Includes index.
    1. Precious stones—Therapeutic use.   2. Crystals—
Therapeutic use.   3. Vital force.   I. Title.
RZ999.C4413 1989   133   88-33756
ISBN 0-87728-694-9

Cover mandala entitled *Infinite Heart* ©Jeanette Stobie, 1989
Used by permission of Lightstream Paintings,
PO Box 3574, Redwood City, CA 94062

Typeset in 12 point Baskerville
Printed in the United States of America

Contents

*This book is dedicated to
the Earth*

Introduction

Let us embark—you and I—into an exploration of the Heart, the human heart, and realize the potential and beauty of our lives.

Many years ago, while living in Sante Fe, New Mexico, I was asked to teach a course, one evening per week, for eight weeks. As I thought of the topics to choose, a small strong voice said "the heart." How was I to do this? The voice said: "Explore." The people who came were interested in self-discovery. Each week we would begin with breathing techniques and movements to help us open and let go of tensions. Then we shared our thoughts, feelings, fears, expectations and discussed myths and stories. And we learned to work through the heart.

My work with healing and teaching has provided me with ample opportunity to experience the depth of the heart in each one of us. So many illnesses have their roots in the heart. People who come to my healing groups are all looking — consciously or unconsciously — to be relieved from old sufferings. Crystals and gemstones have the ability to remove old blockings that constrict the heart, thus allowing a free space to feel the joy and gift of life. But after a crystal healing, you need to maintain the good energy, and working with the heart is one way to keep this energy free.

Healing and opening your Heart is a key to awakening the spirit within. It is through the heart that you see, feel, and touch other people as the reflection of the One. Different colors, cultures, languages, religions, and goals seem to separate us from each other, yet your heart beats with the same longings that other people have — we all need love, contact, warmth.

Once I lived in a community that believed itself to be special, chosen with a unique purpose. I became increasingly aware of the danger of this belief. I realized that my family is not a special group or tribe — my family includes the totality of the human race, as well as the mineral, plant and animal kingdoms.

These last years I have travelled widely while lecturing, teaching, and healing. It has become clear to me that you all begin the healing in your own heart, by opening your heart to yourself first, to see your own beauty and potential. This leads you to feel that you belong here on this wondrous earth, that you are part of this magical universe, at one with the vastness of space, the inexhaustibility of spirit. And it then allows you to love and accept others.

In May 1986, I fulfilled a vision that had come to me in a dream, to organize the first International Healing Conference on Crystals and Gemstones — called Earth, Elements, Consciousness — in Idar-Oberstein, West Germany. It was to be a gesture of gratitude to the Earth for her heart, her love to us. It took place just a few weeks after the disastrous nuclear accident of Chernobyl and the people who came were inspired to manifest their caring. On the last morning we held an offering ceremony and a group of almost two hundred people climbed a hill and formed a great circle. We were each to offer the Earth a prayer, a song, a stone. As I dug the hole, I felt the Earth's life energy on my hands, the sun on my hands and face, and my trusted companion, teacher and friend crystal was by me waiting to be returned to its greater Mother. I felt my heart melting with the greater heart, the cosmic heart, the heart of everyone there. I sensed love to be our only solution and salvation, that we had come to Earth to learn to love.

Today we need to establish a new consciousness on Earth, a heart consciousness which means letting go of the old values, concepts and beliefs that chain and bind us, so we can develop a more cosmic and universal awareness of impersonal love and freedom. I hope this book will help you walk your path until we meet one day in the radiance and warmth of the heart!

—D.S.C.
Munich

Any path is only a path, and there is no affront to oneself or to others, in dropping it if that is the way your heart tells you. . .

Look at every path closely and deliberately. Try it as many times as you think necessary. Then ask yourself alone, one question. . .

Does this path have a heart?

If it does, the path is good; if it doesn't it is of no use.

Carlos Castañeda
The Teachings of Don Juan

Part One

The Heart

1

The Physical Heart

Listen to the heart,
The pulse of life
The cosmic rhythm
Beating and renewing us each moment

The subject of the Heart is so encompassing that we first need to define it physically before we can discuss its ramifications. *Webster's Ninth New Collegiate Dictionary* defines the heart as follows:

1) A hollow muscular organ of vertebrate animals that by its rhythmic contraction acts as a force pump maintaining the circulation of the blood; breast or bosom; something regarding the heart in shape;

2) The whole personality including intellectual as well as emotional functions or traits;

3) The emotional or moral as distinguished from the intellectual nature — generous disposition: compassion, love, affection, courage, ardor;

4) One's innermost character, feelings, or inclinations, e.g., "one after my own heart";

5) The central or innermost part — center, the essential, or most vital part of something; to learn by heart.

This broad definition opens our eyes to this unique and creative organ that is the master of our life and/or death in the body. Its functions encompass the realm of the physical and take us into the realm of feelings, emotions, love, beauty and spirit.

Let's conduct a simple experiment together. Get paper and pen and from the word "heart" follow an association of words or expressions in your mind that represent or use the heart. Please take the time to ponder when making your list; then compare it to mine (shown in Table 1 on page 5) and feel what these words or expressions have meant in your life.

The physical heart is a hollow, four-chambered muscular organ placed between the lungs and enclosed in the cavity of the pericardium. See figure 1 on page 6. The broad attached end (or base) is directed upward to the right and corresponds to the interval between the fifth and eighth dorsal vertebrae. The apex is directed forward and to the left and corresponds to the interspace between the cartilage of the fifth and sixth ribs. In an adult it is about the size of a fist. The upper chambers are called auricles and the lower are called ventricles.

The auricles symbolize the female or intuitive aspect (receiving), and the ventricles represent the masculine (activity or doing). Each half contains elements of the other, thus achieving a totality by sharing each other's polarities. This correlates a belief that American Indians have about "shields" in the heart. For them, an adult male carries in his heart both the boy and the adult man, as well as a little girl and grandmother. An adult woman

Table 1.   Words of the Heart

heart	mercy	sweetheart
life	joy	lion-hearted
death	hearty	heart to heart
love	courage	heavy heart
warm	strength	light heart
hearth	fearless	depth of heart
earth	kind	pink heart
sun	giving	golden heart
cold	blood	heart attack
hate	heartbeat	young at heart
jealousy	rhythm	bleeding heart
anger	drum	heart blessings
tenderness	hero/heroine	heart as altar
softness	heartless	queen of hearts
compassion	heart break	hearts of palm

or,

the heart of the matter,
a sword or knife in the heart,
gratitude in the heart,
"You've got to have Heart" (a song by Frank Loesser).

carries in her heart a little girl, the adult woman, as well as her little boy and grandfather. The heart represents the whole human being.

The Chinese call the heart "the Mother of the blood" because it regulates the flow of the blood. It is the central vessel of exchange and carries animate life. It circulates

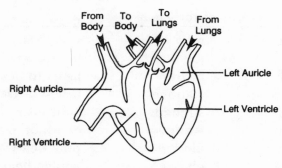

Figure 1. A rough drawing of the heart.

the blood through the blood vessels in all parts of the body, supplying it with nourishing material at the rate of 4,000 gallons a day.

The heart receives the impure blood in the right auricle, passes it to the right ventricle and sends it to be revitalized in the lungs. The left auricle receives the revitalized blood, passes it to the left ventricle and distributes it to the body. This means that both right chambers, auricle and ventricle, have blood which could be called mature (with experience) and both left chambers (auricle and ventricle) have pure (or virgin) blood to circulate back to the body. The vital "Tree of Blood" is the tree of respiration and exchange between interior and exterior.

In the Old Testament (Lev. 17:11) it says, "The LIFE is in the blood." And in the same chapter, 14th verse: "For the life of all flesh is in the blood." The circulation of blood symbolizes a flow, an interchange or sharing — free circulation of all that is required for right human living. Circulation is life, everything alive is in motion, stagnation is death.

The heart and blood are agents of distribution of the life force. The purity and vitality of the whole body depend on that of the blood, but conversely, all the organs cooperate toward its continual regeneration.

The heart is the center and governor of the complete organism. For although the lungs are activated by the air and fire that they breathe in, the heart is the center and motor of the circuit that regenerates the blood in them. It is the agent of combustion of the terrestrial food which is to become assimilable nourishment. The functioning of the organs (stomach, spleen, pancreas, intestine, and kidneys) can be improved through the intermediary of the heart; and the state of the heart depends on the balance of the organs serving it.

Even in its physical functions, the heart is the organ of peace. It is a mediator; by its nature it tries to establish peace and harmony. For example, the heart responds to the aggression of the liver and/or spleen with non-resistance, merely restoring the balance and repairing the damage. The extraordinary power of the heart must be understood so we can appreciate its influence on our total being. One of the best explanations of the heart's functions comes from Dr. Godel, a French cardiologist. In *L'experience Liberatrice* he tells us:

> The heart is engaged in the mysterious work of keeping the whole organism in balance, which is more than just a matter of blood vessels and changing pressures. To correct the effects of injury or disequilibrium, it has remarkable methods of compensation justified by thousands of years of experience. This Wisdom of the Heart has come to us by heredity, as a quality of our species. The heart possesses an ability to repair damage affecting itself without for one moment interrupting the flow of energy it pro-

vides. Thus it is rightly a symbol of unfailing generosity. In the practice of cardiology, we have had to recognize that the heart's power to maintain life is almost unlimited, so long as it is allowed to use its own methods and has unrestricted access to its natural resources. Only too frequently, however, the unfortunate intervention of the psyche, especially in the form of anxiety, turns the course of events into catastrophe. A strong heart, with little damage, has often been known to fail in a few hours under the influence of acute anxiety. One emotional storm can demolish completely the marvellous structure of homeostatic defenses, which, with the Wisdom of the Heart, has come down to us from the depths of time.[1]

The Rhythm of the Heart

Medically speaking, the definition of life is based on the heartbeat, the pulse of life. A few days after conception, the heart begins to develop. In its early stages it is essentially a muscle-wrapped tube that contracts and pushes the blood through itself. These contractions are slow and irregular, gradually accelerating and becoming synchronized to a regular beat. The sounds of the heartbeat are the snapping shut of the valves, first immediately after the auricle where the blood is carried into the ventricle, and second after the ventricles contract and the pulmonic and aortic valves snap shut producing a sharper sound. After

---

[1]Dr. Godel: *L'experience Liberatrice* (Gallimard, Paris 1952), p. 124.

the two sounds there is a brief pause so that the sequence is actually in three parts. The complete cycle is a wave of activity consisting of pulses, muscular contractions and resultant sounds, followed by a pause or silence.

The mother's heartbeat has a strong effect on the developing child. In one hospital experiment, babies were placed in a room where a heartbeat was played through loudspeakers. These babies gained more weight, developed more rapidly, and cried less than babies who did not hear the heartbeat. This rhythm, which is the cosmic universal sound, continues without a break day and night for the duration of our life. It varies in different persons and beats the tempo of our life, be it fast or slow. We cannot stop it, yet emotions — excitement, fear, or passion — can quicken it. Each heartbeat fills us with a realization of existence and with a true understanding of Being.

The great sea of life is swelling and receding, rising and falling. The alternating movement of dilation and contraction is an example of the two powers, both necessary as an act of balance. The earth itself expands and contracts. Dilation is an expansion into oneness, a gesture of union, an absorption into the cosmos. It is without selection, it directs us toward the impersonal. It symbolizes the breaking of boundaries, the fusion of all, the opening of the heart without reserve.

Contraction is the opposite; it symbolizes materialization, personal will, limitation. Each movement is inevitably followed by the other. All things are subject to this alternation. The heart achieves a wonderful balancing act between personal and impersonal.

Listen to your heart for a moment. Simply put your hand over it and feel the pulses or throbs against your breast. One of my favorite ways to listen to my heartbeat is when taking a bath. Put your head in enough water to cover your ears and then listen. It sounds like the beat of a drum. Try it!

The drum is also another way of tuning the self. By playing a drum with a simple beat (or pulse) for a long period of time, you come in contact with the rhythm of the cosmos, and feel a balancing of the self by expressing this rhythmic life force. It must be done consciously, letting the rhythm flow through. You can actually "journey" as the shaman or medicine healer to seek visions.

What makes the heart beat? Ask yourself, for that is the mystery.

2

The Spiritual Heart

Know the flame within the heart
Its purifying fire transforms the Self
Its clear light unites us with the Source

People are beginning to understand more and more that all that exists in the visible world exists as well on an invisible level. The physical organ of the heart is actually the servant of the spiritual heart, the seat of the Presence. Our solar system has an active center, the Sun, whose globe is animated by the invisible sun, the center of all its powers. In turn, the "sun" that vitalizes the physical heart is the spiritual heart, the center of spiritual fire, source of the intelligence of the heart.

Along the dorsal spine, which is the human axis from earth to sky, our column of light, there are seven main energy centers or chakras. These chakras are located in the etheric body or the invisible body. The word chakra derives from the Sanskrit word "wheel" or circle, indicating that the order and the law inherent in these centers is also that of all wheels. The outside of the wheel is kept in place (and in motion) by radiating spokes from an inactive center. Eastern scripture speaks of the entire universe as a giant mandala or spiritual wheel, containing myriads of microcosmic wheels. The vibrations that emanate from each of these chakras have a particular transforming effect on certain bodily parts or organs.

Each of the seven chakras has its external counterpart in one of the major glands of the body. They interact with one another in a most mysterious way. When an organ is not functioning properly, it usually means that the chakra nourishing it is either unbalanced, overactive, or closed.

The Heart Chakra

The Heart Center, or Heart Chakra, is located between the shoulder blades, in the first thoracic. It relates to the thymus gland of the endocrine gland system. It is the fourth chakra and the center for the energies of life. This divine life energy is distributed to the other six major chakras, and then in turn to all the cells and centers of the body.

Its colors are green and pink. Green is the symbol of harmony, sympathy, creativity, health, abundance, of nature in general. It is the merging of yellow (soul) and blue (spirit). Green appears in the spectrum at a balancing point between the first three rays (which are more concerned with the physical aspect) and the last three rays (which relate to the spiritual aspect). Green reaches outward in a horizontal manner, blue reaches upward in a vertical manner. Together they form the cross which is the symbol of life. This color, which is radiated everywhere in nature—in fields and forests—restores and gives new energy.

Pink symbolizes softness, tenderness, affection, love. It is made from red, a color associated with life, courage, and passion, and white, the symbol of light, purity and peace. Thus the red of life softened and purified by the white light.

The heart is viewed as the place of God. In many societies people pledge their oaths by placing a hand upon the heart, as the symbol for truth and love. Mothers carry their babies close to their hearts. The heart exerts a calming influence and unites the heart of the child to the heart of the mother, creating the heart-to-heart link that unites them.

During my workshops many people who are in the process of opening their heart chakra see a flower—very often a rose—unfolding in their heart. All flower symbolism, especially the golden-pink rose, is an expression of unfoldment, of beauty filled with spirit. The physical heart corresponds to the "Heart of the Sun" and therefore to the spiritual source of light and love. It is the center that triggers responsibility and regeneration in the unfoldment of human consciousness. The Chinese call the heart "the Lord and Master of the House." It becomes the organ of intuitive mind, spiritualized feeling, or all-embracing compassion, in which the cosmic abstract is transformed into personal human experience and realization.

Egyptian Mysticism

The Egyptians believed that life is the manifestation of spirit in matter, that life is not limited to physical existence but includes the possibility of a continuous experience in the beyond. This idea of everlasting life relates to the sun's existence. The sun rises each day in renewed strength and vigor, giving life, power, stability, health and joy. The heart (called "ab") is believed to serve the following functions: (1) source of life; (2) fulcrum of balance; (3) conscience.

The heart is not only the seat of power of life, but also the fountain of good and evil thoughts. The word "ab" has a dual meaning for its functions are dual. The physical heart was viewed as the sun in the body, but it also represented the solar-moon principle.

The solar activity in the heart brings movement, energy, substance, form and quality. The lunar passivity is maternal, reflects light, gives understanding. Lunar understanding was considered the consciousness of the heart — the direct conception of what is perceived without analysis, or thoughts of comparison. It is what we call intuition or the wisdom of discernment. When we reverse the letters of "Ab" we get "Ba" which signifies the soul, that which absorbs the universal spirit.

At the time of death, the heart is weighed upon the scale against the feather of the Goddess Maāt to determine the fate of the deceased. Maāt, whose symbol is the ostrich-feather, represents judgment, truth, and law. Metaphysically, she represents equilibrium, essential wisdom, cosmic harmony, universal consciousness, the Consciousness of all consciousness. The individual who is able to acquire awareness of his or her consciousness fulfills and realizes his or her own Maāt, and this highest consciousness is integrated with the universal.

Such a movement (of consciousness) is a movement of return toward the Unity through the elimination of opposition and personal limitations — the Maāt, the good to be sought and acquired during one's existence. It is the way of return, but with the acquisition of consciousness.

If the heart had not been "realized," it was consigned to oblivion to be eaten by Ammit, the devourer. This monster of animal nature was a hybrid symbolized by a crocodile's head, lion's chest, and hippopotamus' hind quarters, which signify the elemental states in which each absorbs what belongs to it — the greed of nature. In other words, having lived as mere matter it dies as mere matter and no more, devoured by Ammit who represents the world of pure carnality uninfused by spirit.

When the death judgment was favorable, the heart was guarded with special care and was mummified separately. It was preserved in a jar; incidentally the hieroglyph for the heart was a jar, which represents the container of life. Preservation of the heart was so important that a text was introduced in the *Book of the Dead* (also called the Book of Great Awakening) at an early period with the intent of providing the deceased with a heart in place of the one which had been removed in the process of mummification.

In Chapter XXVI, "The Chapter of Giving a Heart to the Deceased," the text reads:

> May my heart be with me in the House of Hearts!
> May my heart be with me in the House of Hearts!
> May my heart be with me and may it rest there, . . .
> I shall understand with my heart,
> I shall gain the mastery over my heart . . .

Another verse, from Chapter XXXb, "Not Allowing the Heart of the Deceased to be Driven from Him in the

Underworld," was recited over the amulet of the heart and was often engraved upon it:

> My heart, my mother; my heart, my mother!
> My heart whereby I came into being! . . .
> Let there be joy of heart unto us at
> the weighing of words . . .

The Egyptians reasoned that since the physical heart was taken, and the body needed another to act as the source of life and movement in its new life — or rebirth — another had to be put in its place.

The amulet of the heart was made in the form of a scarab because of the scarab's remarkable power and sacredness. Scarab is derived from the Greek word "scarabeus" which derives from the Egyptian "Khepri." Khepri or Khepera means "morning sun," "he who rolls." It is the transformational nature of Ra, the invisible power of creation which propelled the sun across the sky. It was sacred because it symbolized the following:

1) the principle of the being who produces and achieves successive transformations by itself;

2) the solar principle: it resembles the sun, ascending and descending;

3) the lunar principle: its gestation lasts for twenty-eight days.

The beetle scarab passes through clearly defined stages of transformation in its passage from egg to winged insect. It lays its eggs (or spiritual potential) in a ball of dung (or matter) that it rolls for forty days. During this time, the young pass through the egg, larval, and nymph stages before emerging into the light as winged (spiritual) creatures. The maternal gestating and nourishing environment it creates explains the androgynous character of the legendary scarab.

The amulet, bearer of influences, was put directly over the place of the heart, representing the psychic or subtle heart, which was never to be lost by the deceased, and which underwent the transformation. This symbol of knowledge was made of gold and silver to represent, connect, and integrate the solar and lunar principles. Other amulets were made of black and dark green stone to represent the state of transformation itself. Many scarabs made of green basalt, green granite, light green marble, white limestone and glazed faience of green, purple, and blue colors have been found on mummies. Occasionally the base was made in the form of a heart.

The purpose of the knowledge and recitations of texts at the time of death was to move consciousness and responsibility from the individual to the celestial powers. The Egyptians had a wonderful sense of balance and reciprocity for the gifts of life, prosperity, nourishment, health, light and beauty. The individual gave thanks and used these gifts wisely, indicating a willingness to integrate personality with the Universal consciousness.

Eastern Mysticism

In the Tantric Hindu and Buddhist tradition, the Heart Center is called Anahata Chakra (Sanskrit). It is depicted as a twelve-petalled lotus within a hexagram (or interlaced triangles), and it controls the sense of touch. It represents the element of air and wind, whose characteristic quality is motion. The deer or antelope is a symbol of swiftness and speed and is its vehicle. This element is neutral, acting as a medium between active (fire) and passive (water). Through the interaction of these two the whole created life has become motion. We should not think of the elements only on their grossly material plane, but more as universal qualities.

It is interesting to note that the deer is also the sacred animal symbol for the Huichol people of Mexico and the Zuni people of North America. In many of the Zuni paintings, the deer is represented with light rays coming out of its heart, and with an open passageway from mouth to heart as the life force element is breathed in. The Huichol believe that through dancing "the dance of the deer," one develops and embodies its character traits of strength, agility, gentleness, and tenderness.

The lotus of the heart, which is magnetic in quality and radiating in activity, is believed to represent the principle of "Bhodi" or understanding, the urge to wisdom, compassion, goodwill and peace. It is in this center that the individual is instinctively aware of the joys and sorrows of others, sometimes even reproducing in oneself the physical pain and sufferings of others. It is thought to be like a red flower from which the sound of the pulse of life springs forth.

Two beautiful visualizations we can imagine in the heart are: (1) the Celestial Wishing Tree which grants all one asks for and even more; and (2) the Island of Jewels in the sea of nectar (where the earth is transformed into jewel-like crystals and gems of all colors and brilliance) which is covered with fragrant flowers. Here the devotee becomes like the tree of life whose branches bring forth the fruits of the spirit.

In the Buddhist Tantric system we see a more flexible view of the chakras and their associated elements. These are more detached from their material quality and move on many planes: of nature, the abstract, conceptual, sensual, as well as on the emotional, psychic, intuitional, and spiritual planes. In other words, the Heart Center is to be seen as a red triangle associated with the element fire when used for meditation and reaching consciousness. This red triangle is the fire of inspiration, the psychic fire, the fire of religious devotion. For this reason the heart was compared to the Brahmanical fire — the altar of sacrifice where the sacred flame transforms, purifies, melts, and integrates the elements of the personality.

According to the Tibetan tradition, the energy centers are divided into three zones: (1) upper — the brain and throat; (2) middle — the Heart Center; and (3) lower — the solar plexus and organs of reproduction. In the deepest sense, the upper zone represents the cosmic or universal plane of eternal law, of timeless knowledge, the boundlessness of space, in which form and non-form are equal. The middle zone represents the human plane of individual realization where the forces of Earth and Universe become conscious of the human soul as an everpresent and deeply felt reality. The lower zone represents the forces of nature, materiality, corporeality — the terrestrial plane. We must realize, however, that the heart, which mediates between the upper and the lower centers, and which becomes the realm of realization on the human plane, may only attain these properties through conscious transformation.

The philosophy of the *I-Ching*, the ancient Chinese book on "the principles of nature," is also based on the eternal order and inner relationship of Heaven, Earth and human. By uniting Heaven and Earth within oneself, we each can achieve ultimate harmony and perfection.

To be born as a human being is a privilege, according to the Buddha's teaching, because it offers the opportunity of liberation through one's own decisive effort, through a turning around in the deepest seat of consciousness.

It is in the Heart lotus that tender compassion springs up because of the fusion and sublimation of the two currents, the red (solar force) and the white (lunar force). Knowing and feeling, wisdom and love, brightness of light and warmth of life have become One. All attainment is translated into life and deed. The heart thinks, affirms and unifies. Let us ask ourselves: What has most often guided us? We can say the heart, not the brain or reason.

When I lived in Taos, New Mexico, some years ago, a friend told me a story about Carl Jung, the famed psychologist. One day he went to visit the Pueblo (Indian village) in Taos. He stood with the Elder Chief on the rooftop of adobe houses, looking out into the empty space of the beautiful land. After a time of silence, he turned to the Elder and asked him what he thought was the difference between white man and red man. The Elder replied: "White man thinks with his mind, Red man thinks with his heart." An old maxim reminds us: "As a man thinketh in his heart so is he."

The intelligence of the heart is a vision of the real and communion with it. It is the understanding of the essential nature and quality of the thing. We need to cultivate our intuition in order to perceive the vital qualities of things and beings. To put quality first in anything, in the smallest work, opens your heart to beauty.

3

Symbolism of the Heart

The innermost Heart is
the source of all symbols.

The Heart Center, the fourth chakra, is associated with
the number four which is the symbol of matter, of foundation, of completion, of humanity. Because the number
four is the first result of multiplication, it represents the
principle of becoming and of transformation. We note the
progression of the four kingdoms (mineral, plant, animal
and human) and the four elements (fire, water, air and
earth) which contribute to our make up. Also the four
cardinal points (north, south, east and west) which sur-
round us.

The heart has four chambers, and the foundation of
the pyramid is made up of four sides. The ancient Egyptians recited their prayers four times. They divided the
world into four parts, each corresponding to one of the
four pillars which held up the sky. Each of the directions
or cardinal points was presided over by a special god.
This custom lasted a long time and today the Navajo

people of North America still utilize the four-fold repetition of affirming a phrase which they believe has a magical effect.

In other traditions — Greek texts, the Upanishads, Kabbalistic and Sufi writing — the center within the human being is considered to be the heart. It has been called the seat of Intelligence, of Brahma, of Solomon and of the Universal Logos. The center is the point from which all goes forth and to which all returns, the eternal potential. To be integrated means to be able to maintain contact with your center, your heart so you can realize the source of energy within yourself.

The heart is also seen as a turning point. It is the place where all things meet, and from which all things are possible. It is sometimes represented by an equilateral cross having four equal arms. The cross symbol emphasizes the full extension of your energy, for it discharges both upwards and outwards. The cross as a universal symbol appears in nearly all cultures. The dorje and swastika, as variants of the cross, indicate the rotation of the fire of the heart. Often associated with the idea of motion or change, cross symbolism signifies the path of the sun setting in motion the four cardinal points that move to the center — to each other. Christ, when he declared, "He who would follow me must take up his own cross . . .," was alluding to the significance of the crossroads, asking that we enter into the center of our own being, the heart, so that we might take a new direction. Figure 2 shows some symbols for the heart.

In the Sufi tradition the heart is regarded as winged because it is rooted in the heart of the Creator freed from bondage, filled with spirit, and thus can fly. The Islamic tradition also views the heart as the labyrinth. It creates

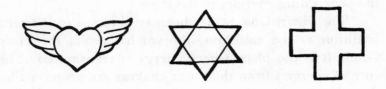

Figure 2. Some symbols for the heart.

and dissolves, expands and contracts, reveals and conceals. It implies death and rebirth, which is the continuous transformation and purification of the spirit throughout life. By the act of circumambulation, which represents attaining the summit, the pilgrim spirals around the Kaaba, the Temple of the Heart, as the Heart of the Universe, as his own heart. The windings are like the turning of the Buddhist wheel of Dharma: the revolutions of the cosmos are seen as the immutable Divine Law. This movement can also be visualized as the cosmic dance, the dance of the planets and the stars, the dance of Shiva. He is the Hindu God, whose dance is the manifestation of primal rhythmic energy — the source of all movement within the cosmos.

The hexagram (or six-pointed star, also called the Star of David) reveals human energy ascending and God (or the creative forces) descending. The point where these energies meet is the point of the Heart Chakra where the flame of life burns. The magnet created within the heart is the ascending triangle which compels the descending triangle. This is the merging of the creator and creation. The star also symbolizes balance and interchange between male and female, the lower triangle representing the receiving energies of the female and the upper triangle representing the penetrating energies of the male.

The Heart Chakra has been symbolized in Western tradition as the cauldron, the witch's kettle, the Holy Grail. It is the place where energy is transmuted. The core of energies from the lower chakras are preserved by the solar plexus and now "leap" into the cauldron. Unless these lower energies are burned in the "flame" of the heart, they cannot reach the higher, more aware, energy centers of the body to be transmuted.

Throughout history, the cult of the heart has existed in all cultures and human beings have performed sacrifices of the human heart. One of the most common to all people was the sacrifice to the Sun. The ancient Mexicans conceived the Sun as the source of all vital life, "He by whom men live." Because the Sun bestowed life on the world, it needed also to receive life from it. Therefore the hearts of men and women were presented to the Sun to maintain its strength and enable it to run its course across the sky.

The Aztecs had a yearly ritual in which a man was chosen for his physical beauty to represent the God of Gods. He was given four brides with names of goddesses: the "Goddess of Flowers," the "Goddess of the Young Maize," the "Goddess of Our Mother across the Water," and the "Goddess of Salt." On the day of his sacrifice, this beautiful young man was dressed in the finest costume, his heart was offered to the Sun, and another "God" was chosen for the next year, thus acting out a ritual expression for the idea of death and rebirth.

Another common theme was the offering of blood to the Earth or crops to insure growth, prosperity and abundance for the village. In several cultures, a warrior or chief would eat the heart of a very brave enemy in order to receive the qualities of courage and valor. The heart was regarded as the supreme power.

The idea behind these ancient sacrifices was that nothing was lost, rather it was transfigured, transformed. It is difficult for us to understand the symbolism of these rituals today. Let us try not to judge them by today's standards.

Truth exists already in our hearts, however ignorant our personalities may be. Pure consciousness, light, the Buddhist principle or the Christian principle, love and wisdom dwell in all beings. It is the voice we hear within the heart, that voice which guides us through the maze of life and influences us to be more responsive to the "heart of all things."

The essentially creative act is the union of opposites for the union of positive with negative results in a raying-out of a new creation. When these polar forces are mutually supportive there can be a terrific release of creative power. All true creation takes place this way. As William Blake is purported to have said: "Without contraries, there is no progression." We live in a world of contrast: man/woman, white/black, day/night, yang/yin, creative/receptive, heavenly/earthly. Everything in nature is a blend of polarities that create a whole. The Tantric image "Yab-Yum" represents the act of sexual union as the ultimate symbol of divine reunion.

Out of the marriage of the light and dark halves of the soul, a wonderful new birth takes place. We are afraid of that which is dark within us, not realizing it is but a shadow of the light and therefore inseparable from it. Ancient myths warn us of the misfortune that pursues the individual who has "lost" the shadow. There is always darkness as well as light. That which we love draws us upward and outward into the light, while that which we hate — the shadow of what we love — draws us backward by its bond of fear. These two forces hold us motionless. We seek to flee but if we would only turn around and face the shadow, everything would change. The nightmare can become a source of inspiration. The American Indians believe that everyone needs to recognize, honor, and dance with the shadow in order to become whole. From the union of light and darkness there arises the sacred flame of the enlightened heart. The Sun shines in the day, the Moon shines at night. But the fully awakened consciousness shines both day and night.

4

Love

All my life
I have been seeking,
seeking!

Unknown American Indian

Throughout the ages human beings have tried to understand the secret of Love. People have looked for it in things, places, people; we have tried to buy it, possess it; we have prayed for it, we've waited all our lives for it, made an art out of it, written about it, sung and danced it, fought and died for it. The wise ones looked inside for it and saw it everywhere.

Love and Life are synonymous. There can be no life, there can be no love without the intertwining of the two. All living is love. You, me, the stones, the plants, the birds, the stars, all, we are all dancing together in the rhythm of life, of love. An invisible thread runs through everything from the Source, from the one common Source.

During a retreat period in the countryside, I lived on a farm. One day I became totally absorbed in watching a mother turkey and her eleven baby turkeys on their first day out in the sun. She moved slowly, showing them what grasses to eat, talking to them continuously to reassure them on their first day of discovery. A divine intelligence was present. She became a teacher to me. The more I watched her in the following days, the more I grew fascinated by her ways. On rainy days, not only her offspring but also chickens would come to her for protection as she spread her wings wide. Her love was full and limitless. The heart opens to a wider dimension when it realizes the creator's divinity in all that lives. We are all children of Creation.

If you can learn to love yourself, the Self will be able to experience trust, acceptance and self-worth. To have faith in your life means to clear away all the obstacles and difficulties, to meet them as challenges and lessons, and to have the courage to let go of safety and security in favor of integrity and individuality. Too much attachment, or depending on others, is not to be encouraged; it is not constructive. It's the reason why so many people are devastated when they lose someone in a relationship and are unable to let go. Your love-ability and your self-worth are not dependent upon external approval. For example, if I am attached to another person because I cannot stand alone, it is not love that I feel, but insecurity. Love is an attitude toward all objects, including the self. It is faith in your potentiality, in your strength, in your love. Recognize your own needs, love yourself enough to fulfill them. Trust in what comes.

We are all starving for love. Love-starvation is even more rampant than food starvation. It invades all classes, all peoples, all climates, every social and economic level. It results in physical and mental illnesses, in delinquency and sometimes even in death. The cry for love is strangled by our social conventions, conditioning, attachments and taboos which cause people to develop defenses and fears.

To live fully means you have to learn to trust. To fear the unknown will impoverish your existence. When you cannot see the outcome, you may not feel strong enough to face life, which means you may settle for a "piece" of life, a seemingly secure place free from dangers or risks. But life demands from you the courage to face the unknown, the marvelous, the inexplicable, the mystical, the wonder of creation.

If you are on the Path there is no escape. On the contrary, the understanding of being human, the acceptance of the value of your life will bring you joy and boundless love. In this process of growth, of coming into being, you must learn to see the double movement — the in-out breath — the outward movement of the warrior (Sun) and the inward movement of the mystic (Moon). The first movement is an outward one — toward evolution characterized by self-assertion on the path of pursuit. The second movement is an inward process, involution, characterized by increasing self-realization in the path of return or union. In most of us the two phases of experience interpenetrate. Both are necessary, as self-realization could never happen without self-assertion.

It is up to each one of you to get in touch physically and spiritually with yourself, to be conscious of every act of indifference, every misuse of life. There are no absolute or final answers. You can move forward if you assume that life symbolizes the activity of the Universe, impelled by Love. This motivating power of Love has always manifested through humanity.

At times you will experience a loss of contact with the knowledge or oneness of life. Sometimes feelings of sadness may come into your heart for no apparent reason, you are changed and don't know how or why. You need to accept these times, to "flow" with them just as a river flows through quiet times and times of upheaval. The more you are silent and patient, and aware of this, the more the unknown will come to you.

Cultivate a love of life for its own sake, let life be, life always has a reason. Be grateful for all your experiences and learn from them. Also learn to accept the movement of your life, to expand and extend yourself. To work towards self-realization is the most important search of all.

Turn Life into a Fountain
It drinks me while I drink it.
Kahlil Gibran

Heaven and Earth, Sun and Moon, man and woman, were originally One. The quest for love lies in overcoming the separateness by experiencing and reaching union. Interpersonal fusion is the most fundamental passion. Desire for sensual love has the same root as desire for truth, the striving for realization. In its lowest form it is like straw fire, nourished by a momentary enthusiasm, while in its highest form, love is the flame of inspiration, nourished by spiritual insight, true vision, direct knowledge and certainty. Both have the nature of fire. This force brings you to truly forget yourself in the transcendence of your own personality. It is an act of self-surrender which frees and transforms your innermost being. It has been called ecstasy, trance, absorption and vision. An old Sufi saying is: "What is Love? Thou shalt know when thou becomest me."

Love is the power that breaks through the walls, the barriers, the images, the conditionings, the masks and unites you with others. This love enables each of you to overcome your sense of isolation, yet permits you to be yourself, and includes all forms of love — parental, fraternal, friendship, romantic, sexual and divine. Yet love can only be practiced in freedom, never as a compulsion. Two become one and yet remain two.

In all Indian mystical literature, the love relation between woman and man is considered to be a reflection of spiritual experience. The two worlds of spiritual purity and sensuous delight need not, and ultimately cannot be divided.

> Let those whose hearts are ablaze with the
> Fire of Love learn courage from this pure Maiden.
> Teach me, O God, the Way of Love, and enflame
> my heart with this Maiden's Fire.

This poem by Muhammed Riza Nan'i was written upon the "suttee" of a Hindu girl whose betrothed was killed on the very day of their marriage. The poet is amazed that after the death of her man, the bride refused to be comforted and wished only to be burnt on the same pyre. When the king heard this he offered the girl protection and wealth, but she refused and he was forced to give his consent to let her burn.

When the Titanic sank, many women refused to be rescued without their husbands or were only torn from them by force. Have you not wished, in the secret of your heart, for a love so pure, so total that would burn bright until your death? Or for the beloved who would rather die than be apart from you? Are these illusions?

If you think of your body as an obstacle on the spiritual path, or if you think of it as an instrument of pleasure or power, when it is mutilated, desecrated or separated from spirit as it has been, the Oneness, the sacredness is lost. In fact, you are cut off from your Source. In the experience of sexual love, or even wisdom, there is no separation between body, soul, spirit, gender, or path. The sacredness is their marriage.

Many non-Christian traditions did not separate the human being into two parts, nor separate the spiritual experience from the lover's experience. The songs and poems of love from the Sufis, the ecstasy of saints — both men and women — the rites of Tantrism, and the erotic symbolism in alchemy all speak of spiritual realization. Remember the Hermetic statements: "all is in all" or "above as below." Here you find no contradictions.

> Looking deep
> Into the well of feelings
> See how
> Bodies dissolve
> In a single form
> Unite in One
> For one great revelation
> Love . . .

Chandidas wrote this poem. He was a rebel poet priest from Bengal. He had a vision of the Goddess, who said to him that he was to love a beautiful young woman from a lower caste, but that he was to conquer the temptation of the senses and to make love the "Sahaja" way. This path relates to yoga and means "union," but unlike the yoga you might be familiar with, it uses tension as a means for imparting consciousness. Instead of suppressing what is regarded as weakness, it exploits it in order to be free from it. Great emphasis was laid on freedom from possession, which was regarded as pollution. The body was viewed as sacred, and the state of being in love was considered as a state of being aware of existence itself—of alertness to each vibration of life.

The love of Radha and Krishna unlocked a tidal wave which flooded all of India for over five hundred years, blending divine love with sensual fervor, religiousness with poetry, music, and painting. The mood of these love songs reflects the spirit of Bhakti. The Bhakti Path is a path of devotion; it is like the love of a lover who is free from any motive other than the very act of loving, of giving of himself. This love for the Creator is beautifully expressed in the following:

> I gave in full
> My love, my life, my soul, my all.
> Mira Bai

Jalulah Dīn Rúmi from Konya, Turkey, considered one of the greatest mystics, wrote:

> The prophet of God said: "Men are as mines";
> the self is a mine of silver and gold and is
> truly full of gems.
> Discover yourself . . .
> Fill your heart with hope, and polish it well
> and clear, for your pure heart
> is the mirror of the sun of splendor.

Love is your heritage; it is the flower of humanity; it is the perfume for one and all. A flower exudes a scent, whether you appreciate it or not. Love gives you the opportunity to mature, ripen, take form, to become yourself a world — whole.

Love from one human being to another is the most difficult test, the highest witnessing of yourself. It is the Supreme Act between two solitudes, caring, complementing, moving back and forth, one in front of the other. It is possible only when the two communicate from the center of their existence, from their hearts.

If I meet you as someone apart, someone I don't like or someone who doesn't like me, I am making a barrier between us. But if turning away from everything that appears limited, we meet each other as Divine Beings, this will also include us as humans. The greater includes the lesser. When this is not happening it is because your unconscious denial is choking it. You need to quietly affirm the limitless abundance of Love.

As you look ahead into the present time, you'll notice the transition from the Piscean era, which was symbolized by two fishes swimming in opposition, to the awakening of the Aquarian age, symbolized by the pouring path of equal, fraternal love. The Aquarian age brings new roles for both men and women. Perhaps you can incorporate and integrate the primal archetypal roles of God and Goddess to reach individual harmony. Remember that each one of you carries the principle of the other. The male carries the principle of the female and the female carries the principle of the male. Thus you can become not only lovers but brothers and sisters, loving passionately and tenderly. Love means complete giving, in the sense of an unlimited expansion of yourself into Universal

Self. It wants nothing but to radiate, giving impersonally, unconditionally, just as the sun radiates on each and all alike. The final goal is to be LOVE.

Compassion and Love

"Feel the consciousness of each person as your own consciousness," said Shiva to Pavarti. Along my path to awareness and love, a teacher gave me the name Daya as a daily, living reminder. In Sanskrit, Daya means Compassion. In the depths of my heart the name resonated to what I knew was an essential aspect of love. Love is enormous compassion.

Compassion — with passion — a passion for all, for everything. Passion is not personal. There is no creation without passion. It is a communion with all, from the heart the Self merges with the universe and embraces all. It begins in your own heart. Look inside, look at the roots to understand the content of your consciousness. In this understanding of yourself flowers wisdom, which is the knowledge of the essential quality and unity of all beings. It is not sentimentality but the recognition of another's being and value.

This movement leads you naturally to a deeper perception of the world around you. You begin to empathize and sympathize by letting go of moral judgments, of good and evil, of condemnation and blame, of wanting to be righteous, of control mechanisms, of the I.

Empathy is the perception of an object in terms of its nature, movement and tendency. The object is "felt" — the branches of the tree are "felt" to be swaying in the wind, the sea is "felt" to be rushing and exploding against the cliff or shore. This experience involves your imagination and opens your heart and eyes to seeing in a new light. Through the ability to see more and more aspects of the many-sidedness of a person or thing, the perceiver and the perceived become more like each other as they both move toward unity. This unity has the flavor of love, life and beauty.

In its unconscious drive for security and continuity the family unit has established strong patterns of habit and tradition. Here lie the roots of tribalism and racism which have created separation and conflicts. In your journey through life, you must overcome the neurotic attachment of being the child of somebody and the citizen of only one country. You belong to the World, the Universe. Krishnamurti said in one of his lectures: "If you are attached, don't try to be detached, it will make you hard and callous. Detachment breeds callousness. Another feeling must come in, one of total trust, love without fear."

The Buddha taught that those who seek compassion must themselves be compassionate to every being alike without special favor. He himself learned by living and became an Enlightened One. His power to reach the heart of every living being with the rays of his boundless compassion, his infinite capacity to participate in the joys and sufferings of others, without being torn or swayed by them, established the inner contact with all that lives.

Bhodi means "awake" and "citta" means heart — "awakened heart" comes from being willing to face yourself. How often do you connect with your heart truly and fully? How often do you turn away because you fear to discover something terrible about yourself? How often do you shield, protect or defend yourself? If you have fears you can also go beyond them and be fearless. Courage and bravery are born in the heart. If you are not afraid of facing yourself, you have the courage to become a warrior. Warrior means "who is brave," man or woman, not in the sense of aggression toward others, but in assisting and helping, being heroic and kind.

These principles of warriorship were embodied in the cultures of India, Tibet, China, Japan, Korea, in the Americas North and South, in the Western Christian societies embodied by King Arthur and also the Jewish King David. This wisdom of fearlessness and rejoicing, in appreciation for life, is a tradition that does not belong to any culture or religion.

Gentleness, tenderness, even sadness are necessary qualities for a warrior who must keep his or her heart open and raw. The heart is purified through suffering and compassion, in the knowledge of the unity of the human being and the cosmos. Offer yourself to the world so you can serve and rejoice in deep reverence. In the delightful and meaningful story of the Little Prince by Antoine de St. Exupéry, after the fox and the Prince have become friends, the fox wants to give the Prince a secret as a parting gift. "Here is my secret. It is very simple: We only see rightly with the heart. The essential is invisible to the eyes."

To see with the heart means that each perception becomes unique. In the warrior, the Sun has entered and merged with his or her heart, radiating its brilliance and extending to others. There is no limit to the manifestation of love; it is the Healing Power of the Heart.

Beauty as Love

Many of the great philosophers—Goethe, Blake, Schiller—believed that beauty is timeless, that reality and truth are found in the experience and that the capacity to feel beauty is not to be acquired through study but is a gift, a blessing and a grace. Goethe said, "For beauty they have sought in every age He who perceives it is from himself set free."

In the creative act you can attain states of absorption, trance, ecstasy in which a union is achieved between the creator and the created as in dance, music, painting, writing or whatever form it may take. According to the poet-writer-philosopher Rilke, beauty arises in works of art, not necessarily from the object seen, but from the depth of the artist who felt in his heart the necessity to express it.

In a creation of beauty exists an element or principle of devotion which causes your heart to soar into flight. A painting or a dance may look lovely but unless it is open or exposed, it is empty. I remember once during a dance class, my teacher came over to me, touched my heart and said: "Dance only from here, do not concern yourself with what the movement looks like." This made a deep impression on me which has influenced my view of dance. To dance you must feel like a child in the joy of pure movement. Dance is the wholeness of the body in tune with the heart and the life force. For me dance is a way to restore balance in my body, to come in tune with the rhythmic energy of the Earth and the cosmos and to liberate myself from the blocks of energy which create depression, and false boundaries or concepts in the Self.

The more complete your identification, the more intense and ecstatic is your experience. To realize the essential unity, the fountain of creative energies in and through oneself, is the basis of self-renewal.

To the artist, lover, or philosopher, spirit and matter are one. Form that awakens an aesthetic emotion in your heart is called beauty, and exhibits the inner relation of things. Beauty gives pleasure to the senses and exalts the spirit. The heart, as the throne of consciousness through its refinement, senses beauty; it thrills and quivers. Beauty may be discovered anywhere and everywhere. Stones are for me incredible objects of beauty, whether from the sea, the river, or the mountain, for their patterns and form speak of patience and eternity. A gemstone filled with color and light is an old enduring symbol of the Earth. Very often their designs show cosmic forms such as spirals, circles, or eyes. They capture rainbows and all at once my heart leaps in joy at the wonder of the spectrum. I rediscover truth and beauty, my heart expands in admiration.

The vision of beauty is spontaneous. It is a state of grace that cannot be achieved by deliberate effort. The beauty in stones, plants, animals, people is naked in love. By appreciating your connection to the brilliant blue sky, the freshness of green fields, the movement of the sea, the vividness of colors in flowers, the play of light in gemstones, the gentleness of a breeze, the brilliance of a sunrise or sunset, you can actually heal yourself and walk the Path of Beauty.

> In beauty I walk
> With beauty before me I walk
> With beauty behind me I walk

With beauty below and above me I walk
It is finished in beauty
It is finished in beauty
Let all hearts be glad

Navaho

The Path of Beauty has opened my heart to a way of life. It means to be whole, to be healthy and self-healing, to be attuned to the great forces of the Universe, to acknowledge praise and give thanks, to be humble in the face of all life, and most of all to love this Earth for all she has given to us. It is a path of nature, a complete spiritual concept in union of matter and spirit manifesting the absolute. It is like being able to extend your being in all directions and having an immediate meaning.

What is beauty? A pleasing movement? A harmony of proportions? A melody that touches your heart? A flavor you taste? A charming trait? A physical attraction? An intensity of power? Plato said: "Everyone choses his love out of the objects of beauty according to his own taste." This relativity is well suggested in the story of the famous lovers Laila and Manjun when it was pointed out to Manjun that the world at large didn't regard Laila as beautiful. He answered: "To see the beauty of Laila requires the eyes of Manjun."

The more you consider the variety of cultures, the more you must understand the relativity of taste. And yet absolute beauty exists. Absolute beauty is identified with the divine; every natural object is an immediate realization of this divinity. There are no degrees in this beauty — can you say that a bird is less beautiful than a horse? The most complex and the most simple expression can remind you of the unity of your being. The heart as the beautiful is the recipient of grace, the realization of the source.

In ancient Egypt, the Goddess of love, beauty, music, dance, and gaiety was Hathor. She was depicted as the celestial cow who provided great spiritual nourishment and healing. The Greeks later equated her to Aphrodite/Venus (Roman)—Goddess of Love and Beauty who is said to have sprung from the sea. This laughter-loving goddess was described as moving in radiant light, bringing joy and loveliness wherever she was, piercing the hearts of men and gods alike. Her son was Eros (or Cupid) and her great beloved was Adonis. Her symbols were the myrtle tree, the dove and sometimes the swan and the sparrow. To this day these are still regarded as symbols of love and beauty and, in the case of the dove, peace.

We cannot achieve beauty, we can only open as the Lotus opens its petals until its golden heart reflects the brilliance of the Sun. Limitless is the beauty of the Cosmos, when by the way of our heart we can penetrate into the consciousness of the Cosmic breath, the Cosmic Heart. The Heart, our treasure chest, our most beautiful jewel, is to be opened to the totality of experience where a vision of immense splendor and beauty is ours to manifest. As Roerich wrote: "In beauty we are united, through beauty we pray, with beauty we conquer."

5

Emotions

Emotions lie deep —
Hidden volcanoes and underground seas!
Go past your images and masks.
Transform the fire
Into food for the spirit

We live in an amazing age. We've made miraculous technical advances. We've put people on the Moon. Yet on our own planet we continue to act like barbarians. We fear our global neighbors; we arm ourselves against them and they against us. We *say* we are thinking of *survival*. But hasn't the time come to *really* survive? Isn't it time to remember we are all human beings?

If you are to develop your heart center, you need to recognize your emotions. You cannot suppress them; you need to transform them. And you cannot transform something you don't consciously understand. One way to understand your feelings is to keep a journal.

My journals have been allies, for there I could express all my feelings and then step back to observe, question and answer myself. They have saved my sanity and have shown me my weaknesses, my dependencies, my attachments, my patterns, my conditioning and my excuses. They have opened my eyes and my heart time and time again to stop the self-punishments, the judgments, the criticisms, the guilts to allow me to have patience in the face of what is still unresolved. Somewhere deep inside I knew that I was not to stifle my passions in my journal for how else would I recognize the forces in me that needed to be transmuted?

By taking a stand towards acquiring consciousness, my sense of responsibility grew. By working with my journal, I could get rid of obstacles toward transformation. I could learn how my sentimental emotions came out of personal motives and I could see how they were not in contact with spiritual realities. I found that through a sudden moment of awareness or a sorrow overcome, I could see the reality of a condition and joy would come into my heart. This quiet joy of release is the consciousness of the cosmic human being. It is the liberation from personal limitations, the expansion of the heart.

We are not born rational beings, we are emotional beings with incredible potential to transform everything around us. We are human transformers, physical transformers. We unconsciously transform air, water, and food into blood, bones, muscles, etc. We can be intellectual transformers, too. All that we see, hear, and study can be transformed into ideas, actions, a philosophy for our lives. We can also be emotional transformers as we learn to transform our feelings. Our emotions have the power to change our body chemistry. Our doubts, fears, attachments, dependencies, greeds, lusts, all these poisons can be transformed into instruments of knowledge and choice. In *Hamlet*, Shakespeare said: "Give me that man that is not passion's slave, and I will wear him in my heart's core, ay, in my heart of heart . . . "

Emotions are powerful, vital, and highly significant forces. They control, disturb, and reveal our state of health, our view and way of life, the traumatizing conditioning of our childhood and the cause of negativity within our behavior. They create distinctive patterns of color and form in the human aura, which are visible to those with the ability of clairvoyance. (Clairvoyance is the capacity to see beyond the normal range of sensory perception.) Each thought or emotion causes corresponding vibrations accompanied by colors. The quality of thought determines the color — radiant and clear for positive emotions, dull and muddy for negative emotions.

Our tensions are largely the result of not knowing how to direct and transform energy. In the next chapters we will explore methods for releasing and transforming. These tensions bring on illnesses and sufferings, yet a certain amount of tension is necessary to bring positive changes. We need to learn the principle of transformation; to learn how to transform energy from a negative emotion into a positive action. Instead of being the passive victim of a situation, we can become its master. External events have no fixed value. We must choose whether to disregard them or to respond to them. However our deep inner being should remain unaffected by them.

There are several factors to be considered when we learn to control our emotions. One very important consideration is that we take ourselves so very seriously, with so much self-importance, that we become very quickly offended and take everything personally. On the other hand, we do not allow other people to experience their negativity. We take it on and then usually pass it on to someone else or become depressed. Another important factor, already mentioned but needing to be said over and over again, is the attachment we carry to the image or role we are caught in playing—mother, father, business person, intellectual, wife, husband, etc. As we are confronted with our images, we react to preserve them, to defend them. We fall in the trap of clinging to our past conditions and behavior patterns.

Sensitive people who are rich in feelings are often also vulnerable—a word, an inflection, a tone, a silence, a look, a gesture, even a color or sound—might be felt as pain, hurt, offense, rejection, humiliation, the end of a relationship. We need to learn not to identify with the I as in "I am in pain," but rather to acknowledge that when there is pain, it will pass. Let us be careful what we attach to "I," for the mind believes it and takes on whatever the situation or problem is.

We have the choice of responding or of reacting to others. When we react we are lost in our emotionality. We can only be in charge of our emotions by becoming more conscious of what is going on at the moment. Do not suppress or run away! A storm is not to be feared but experienced. The atmosphere is charged with energy, let it come in, let the energy help in making the changes that are necessary for growth. Ask: "What am I experiencing?"

We should not be disheartened by our imperfections but need to rise up with fresh courage. Patience is not to be developed only for others but for ourselves! To make a fresh beginning daily and never think we have done enough is one way to attain courage and self-esteem. If we worry and fret over our failings, we will be unable to correct them. If we are impatient with ourselves, how are we to be patient with our mates, neighbors, relatives or friends? How are we to achieve wisdom and inner strength? When we lose patience our hearts founder in emotion, then we can no longer self-analyze, or observe — we are caught.

Throughout the ages, tragedy and comedy have been used to reflect the emotions of people. In the mystery plays of ancient Egypt, Greece and Tibet, the representation of the highest virtues was interwoven with the appearance of demonical or diabolical figures and/or clowns. Far from destroying the juxtaposition of the sublime or the ridiculous, the effects rather seem to deepen the sense of reality in which the highest and the lowest have their place and condition each other. Tragedy and comedy are forever interwoven in the events of our life. Seriousness and a sense of humor do not exclude each other. On the contrary, they indicate the fullness and completeness of experience and the capacity to see the relativity of all things — especially our own position.

I remember attending sacred dances in Indian pueblos and among the dancers there would appear the most grotesque clowns weaving in and out of the solemn circles, gaping into the faces of the participants, defying and ridiculing the sacredness and seriousness. The dancers, however, never seemed to mind and continued with imperturbed dignity. It is the element of the contrary, the opposite, so well understood in these cultures that helps keep life in balance.

Don Juan tells Carlos Castañedas in *The Teachings of Don Juan* something I need to remember daily: that he never gets angry any more at anyone because no one can do anything important enough! We get angry at another person when we feel that his or her behavior is important. The more we make other people important in a negative sense, the more we are dependent on them. When we feel dependent, we also feel rage, envy, jealousy, etc., because the other has the power to remove "it" for us. This "it" is security, in whatever form it takes. Rage, envy and jealousy have driven people to destroy themselves. These negative emotions are the chains that blind us to freedom and love. We think that we have to clutch, protect, even to possess. For example, I have experienced jealousy. It is a pain that paralyzes me with anger first, then fear and distrust, and which takes my power away. Then I feel guilty because of the anger I felt toward my beloved. We all do this. It creates a cycle of negative and destructive emotions. We have given up our power, we feel weak, with low self-esteem, and we become depressed. It is important to understand the emotion, so it can be transformed.

Greed is another poison. We keep buying, eating, drinking, or taking from the natural resources of the Earth in order to fill this emptiness that we feel. It will never be satisfied until we look at it and decide that we no longer want to be controlled by it.

Envy colors everything that we experience with an ugly feeling. It is what the other has that we want, or so we think. We envy a dress, we envy the neighbor's car, we envy the vacation someone else takes, we even envy the spiritual progress of a friend! This envy makes us wish to devalue, or negate or even destroy what somebody else has.

As we acquire a sense of humor we cannot but be compassionate in our hearts, because our sense of proportion allows us to see things in their proper perspective. Our physical senses give us a knowledge of the whole universe, of its fullness and splendor. Guilt, and fear and negativity only spoil the beauty that is here for us.

Fear is the product of thought, the thought of losing, of aloneness, of insecurity. If there is fear there is no love. It distracts our thinking, it makes us bitter and anxious, and it closes the flow in our hearts. When we lose something or someone, it is very painful. We need to allow ourselves to grieve for it. To have a period of mourning is very important, it enables us to go on and greet the future.

The courage to be our own person demands our rejection of mass-produced thoughts. We need to appreciate quality versus quantity. We need to be unattached to any single aspect of ourselves or of our lives, to learn to let it go.

By arousing in our hearts the power of light and of spiritual awareness, the miracle of transformation takes place and we can progress to being able to see things face to face, as they are, without attachments and without aversion. Inner darkness — or ignorance — is the root of suffering. The more the inner light comes, the more the darkness will diminish and we can cultivate positive emotions such as solidarity, gratitude and joy.

Positive emotions uplift, enlarge and exalt the heart. There are thousands of opportunities to experience joy and then be thankful, thus multiplying its value. To acknowledge a thing learned or received is to reflect it within the self and treasure it as a gift. Einstein expressed that beautifully when he said, "The most beautiful and most profound emotion we can experience is the sensation of the mystical . . . He to whom his emotion is a stranger, who can no longer wonder and stand in rapt, in awe, is as good as dead."

Part Two

Healing

6

Healing and Opening

When all the knots of the heart are unloosened,
then even here, in this human birth,
the mortal becomes immortal.
This is the whole teaching of the scriptures.
Kathopanishad II 3, 15

The foundation of health and healing is the inseparable unity of the spiritual and the material. Thus the key to living is a constant intuition of the unity of all life. The Buddha once said to his disciple Ananda: "If you wish to untie a knot, you must first find out how the knot was tied for he who knows the origin of things also knows their dissolution."

To integrate the spirit, heart and body consciously requires energy and work. Gold and precious stones look quite ordinary before they are polished and cut, yet the knowledge of their existence induces people to spend tremendous efforts to find the stones in their raw state. Similarly, you must exercise your consciousness, your awareness, continuously in order to discover your own inner treasures. Nothing can be done absent-mindedly. You need to train your attention so you can observe the smallest, and thus you will understand the greatest. The heart, a manifestation of universal consciousness, is to be vigilant. A dormant heart leads to decay. The heart hardens when you live by habit. Habits are the callouses of the soul. Have you not been aware of the warning of your heart? Does it not quicken its pulse before you lie or do something hurtful? Pause a moment and return to your childhood, try to remember your heart.

Thoughts are the sources of your knots and illnesses. You need to rise above your own thinking, to make a conscious decision to be awake and responsible for yourself. Blaming others is falling unto unconsciousness; self-pity is poisonous. You lose your center when you attack, argue, or defend yourself. Everyone has an urging compulsion to be right, but you need to learn to take two steps back if you are to walk the spiritual path. Thoughts accompanied by feelings and emotions affect your heart and body. Each thought gives birth to action and you need to remind yourself that intuition is equal to action.

If you live with thoughts of a depressing nature, your body will respond likewise, but if you maintain a mental attitude of health, strength, and fearlessness, you will manifest these qualities accordingly. Everyone has experienced obsessions, compulsions, or uncontrolled emotions which have brought on nervous derangements. Negativity, fear, hatred, greed, and an unforgiving heart cause many physical disorders. By learning to trace the condition back to the beginning, you learn the origin of the condition.

Fear is often directly or indirectly at the bottom of many emotional and physical complaints. Many clients tell me of a fear of loneliness, fear of having obligations, fear of being caged-in, fear of loss of beauty or youth, fear of emptiness in life or work, fear of uncertainty of the future or the unknown, fear of poverty, or of having to arrange for oneself, and the final fear—fear of death.

Worry is a magnified form of fear, a thought which torments the heart, a fixation of attention. Fears and worries need to be replaced with confidence and courage, for the physical results will follow. Even the most tender and compassionate heart should not be lacking in courage. Cheer, hope, joy, and a desire for health and happiness give growth to health in general.

Love is the healer, the eternal bond, the binder of hearts, the bread and the wine, the gold. When you make this connection, you can transform yourself into what you can be. This process of transformation is the healing necessary to the Opening of the Heart.

Remember to accept yourself and nurture yourself. It is not enough for others to love you. Love can be given to you but you cannot truly receive it until you love yourself. Decide to become the best channel of "heart" that you can be. Release yourself from guilt and forgive. To forgive means to free one another from bondage. To forgive you must be free of fear, conceit, deceit, envy, jealousy, self-pity, remorse, ingratitude, free of self-condemnation and self-hatred. Try forgiving one situation at a time, for then you will learn how to do it.

To begin the healing process you need to accept illnesses as symbols of various blocks, emotions gone sour into criticisms of others and self. Everyone knows that heart troubles and many other physical disorders are caused by anxiety, worry, nervousness, lack of love, loss of love, feelings unexpressed or suppressed, or frustration. People die from broken hearts when overcome by sorrow. Blood disorders also may indicate a lack of love for self, for others, or for the spirit. High and low blood pressure, leukemia, diabetes all cry out that love is all there is. You need to give love, or your systems get poisoned. Problems with the throat or voice are connected to the heart. Are you expressing truth? Your true self? If you are overweight, it indicates a lack of self-love, even hatred, so you compensate for this lack by putting in your mouth or belly enough food to fill the emptiness. You can also hide your beauty or potential with a swollen, distorted body. Your hands and arms, which are extensions of your heart, symbolize giving to yourself and others, the faith or the loss of touch. Everyone is burdened to some extent with old sufferings which have left their scars on our hearts.

We need to see each other again, to see fellow human beings as the incredible potential for self-healing and love.

Silence and Solitude

Silence is the well of wisdom and inspiration, it contains all treasures. It is by going in the silence that you can face much of yourself. As St. John of the Cross said, "It is in silence and work that transformation is brought to completion." Times of retreat are immeasurable gifts on the path to self-understanding and comprehending your own heart. Solitude is heavy to bear for most people, yet it is necessary to go within, to be alone, to see the thoughts and memories that arise. What goes on inside merits attention and love. In times of retreat, especially in a natural setting, you can observe the wonders of the universe and the wonders of your heart in quietude. You can find communion in nature, in the still nights, in the wind, in the trees. You can watch a butterfly or listen to a bird. Your deeper consciousness will awake and will know.

Rejoice and be grateful for these moments, for it is then that you are in tune with the love all around you.

Take the time to sit in silence and if your heart wanders, bring it back gently. And even if you did nothing during the whole of your hour but bring your heart back, though it went away every time you brought it back, your hour would be well employed.

As I have practiced this myself, I am aware of distracting and disturbing thought patterns that arise in the mind and in the heart. These deal with fears and worries — such as the fear of being totally alone with yourself. Being alone with yourself means to confront your innermost needs — the need to be heard, the need to be touched, the need to be accepted. Also, old painful memories may rise. Childhood memories, which, because they have been repressed, create negative, often angry and violent emotions in the self or toward others.

Feelings of restlessness may also come in because you are so used to doing something physical that you may feel you are wasting time, you wish to be doing something, anything. When you come in touch with your rage, anger, fear, pride, greed, self-importance, vanity, control, you cannot bear them and may wish to hide from these poisons. But when you finally accept the situation as it is and you can say, "Yes, I am here, I am not running any place, I am with myself, I see what I do . . .," then all changes. Acceptance and transformation has set in and you find your heart connecting to the Greater Heart. All at once you do not feel alone. You feel and are aware of your vertical connection with the Earth, the sky, the stars. One of the most important keys is to be true to your own nature. Thus by taking the time to connect with yourself, your essence, your heart, you come into your center and realize the source of energy within yourself. Through this process of transformation, self-healing and love take place and harmony and peace come to you as rewards.

Enter your heart, your center. In the center there is silence.

Self-Suggestion and Affirmation

The power which imagination exercises in life and health was established long ago. Any conscious idea, thought, or feeling will alter and affect your condition. Good suggestion is capable of restoring your health and way of being. Begin by consciously affirming the limitless abundance of love. True abundance is a consciousness of oneness and quality, not separation and quantity. Make self-suggestions, speak to yourself. Tell yourself how you would like to be. Visualize yourself in health and harmony. For example: "I am getting stronger, I see and feel love around me, there is beauty in my life." Right thinking shifts your consciousness. You must do that if you wish to be well. One way that helped me was to write affirmations which were positive statements. If you write an affirmation a hundred times, or a thousand times—whatever you need—you will eventually believe it. A teacher once made me write the following until I couldn't write anymore: "I accept joy in my life and I let go of old sufferings." Your thoughts today affect tomorrow. The heart responds to loving instructions. Next time your heart quickens in emotion or palpitates in fear, place your hand gently over it and speak to it softly: "Quiet, quiet, quiet now my heart." It will respond and gradually quiet down. There is intelligence in every part of your being.

Right Diet for Right Living

In my quest for health I learned the importance of right diet and the use of foods as natural medicine. Many basic causes of heart disease can be traced to faulty eating and living habits and, as we have explored, to mental and physical environmental stresses. Wrong diet causes impure blood and weakens the heart. A lack of exercise and poor circulation adds to this. The blood, which circulates through every cell in the body, if pure and alkaline, will dissolve and carry away poisons. No disease can exist in pure blood, so it is very important to flush and cleanse the body regularly in order to eliminate excess acids and mucus. These are the principal causes of disease and the aging factor.

Each one of you must at some point decide to do away with over-indulgences in food, alcohol, coffee, tea, sugar, or white flour. You may want to eliminate meat and animal fats and replace these with lots of natural foods, such as vegetables, fruits, seeds, nuts, whole wheat bread, juices and herb teas. Twice a year I do a cleansing diet which means eating lots of citrus fruits—oranges, grapefruits, lemons, one raw salad at lunch, and one cooked vegetable meal at dinner. Sometimes I do a diet of only green foods: green vegetables such as zucchini, cucumber, celery, all green salads, sprouts and green fruits, as well as green apples, green grapes. Remember "green" for the heart, green is healing and cleansing. I have also experimented with different fasting methods for one day, three days, seven days, or fourteen days. I recommend the concept of a day fast once a week, or periods of three to seven days in summer, especially if you are in the country and can get lots of fresh air.

Vitamin E given in great doses has helped many with heart problems. You may wish to pursue this idea with your doctor. Walking, jogging, riding a bicycle or horse, swimming and my own favorite, jumping rope in the fresh air, are extremely beneficial both as preventive and therapeutic measures. This advice is not new. In Psalms 104:14 it says: "To make the blood stream pure and health producing eat food in its natural state as far as possible, drink freely of pure water, bathe frequently, exercise in pure air and sunshine and use non-poisonous herbs that were given for the service of man."

Yoga

Yoga means union—union of spirit with physical, and union of self with Self. Yoga is a key that helps open the door so you can experience different levels of consciousness, so you can expand yourself. Expansion of your identity will change your relationship to the universe, your values will change and you will feel differently about the people in your life. When you invite a change, you also effect changes in others, and your circumstances change. Equilibrium, harmony and unity are experienced through purification.

The following postures, exercises and movements stimulate, strengthen and open the heart chakra. Keep your attention on your heart and breathe deeply and slowly. Imagine that you breathe in white light on the inhalation and release darkness and negativity during exhalation. You may experience physiological changes, for example you may perspire more, exuding toxins from your hands and chest. You may also feel an acute blockage of energy flow at your neck. These are normal reactions when working and stimulating the heart center. It is a good idea to do some deep breathing, followed by stretching your body before beginning the following yoga postures. Stretch up on your toes, reach for the sky, stretch forward, stretch down to your toes and stretch backwards—listen to your body and stretch it wherever it needs to be stretched.

1) While standing, with arms parallel to the ground, elbows at ninety degree angles to your arms, hands in a mudra (hand position) where the thumb and index finger are together, begin running in place, on your toes. This is wonderful for the circulation. Do this for at least five minutes. See figure 3.

Figure 3

2) Sit in a comfortable meditation posture. Pay attention to the regular energetic flow of your breath. Feel your own radiance and light. Then join your palms together at your heart center, thus joining the Sun and Moon energies, the right and left side of the body, creating a balance within. Keeping your palms together,

Figure 4

begin long deep breathing for at least three minutes, focusing your concentration on the beat of your heart. See figure 4.

3) In same sitting pose, place
your right hand, palm down,
on your chest at the heart center. Place your left hand palm
up on your back, just opposite
your right hand. Feel the flow
of energy between your hands.
As you inhale and exhale

Figure 5

deeply, concentrate your ener-
gy at your heart center for five minutes. Then relax by
lying on your back. See figure 5.

4) Sit with your legs straight
out, toes pressed forward,
arms straight out in front of
your body, parallel to the
ground with your hands at eye
level. Then bring your legs up
so they are parallel to your
arms and breathe rapidly for
one to three minutes. Repeat

Figure 6

this several times. This exercise affects not only your
heart and circulation, but also your solar plexus and nervous system. See figure 6.

5) Camel pose. Sit on your
knees, reach back and grab
your heels, arching your waist
up and forward. Breathe
deeply for one to three minutes. This exercise opens your
heart center and affects the
navel point and fourth verte-
bra. See figure 7.

Figure 7

6) Cobra pose. Lay on your stomach, bring your arms and hands to shoulder level, then gently raise your torso up on your arms and lift your head back. Breathing deeply, focus on your heart and the third eye. See figure 8.

Figure 8

7) This pose can be done while sitting, or on your knees, or even when standing. With your spine perfectly straight, stretch your arms at a sixty degree angle, with your palms facing up. Make the sound ahh, ahh, ahh, which is the sound of the opening of the heart. Feel your-

Figure 9

self lifting upward, opening and receiving the radiance of universal love. Then do a deep relaxation on your back, arms and legs totally stretched out. See figure 9.

Heart Meditation

The first step involves making an intense effort to identify your own heart, the little heart with the Greater Heart or the Heart of the Cosmos, your own source of life with the cosmic source of all light and life. This is not a sug-gestion — this is an identification or direct communication with reality.

1) You may sit on a chair or in a yoga position. Allow yourself to become physically comfortable. Breathe deeply a few times and mentally relax your body. Watch your thought patterns with detachment as they fly around aimlessly. As these thoughts become still, concentrate your attention quietly on your heart, and the region between the heart and solar plexus. This is the physical correspondence to the Spiritual Heart.

2) Let yourself be penetrated by the peacemaking power of your physical and spiritual heart and trust its full effect.

3) Put aside all feelings of anxiety, negativity, or pessimism which would prevent any such communion. If this is too difficult, if too much negativity arises, then consciously bring it to your heart to be purified and cleansed.

Remember, the heart's tendency is to make peace by balancing and bringing harmony as well as by purifying. This meditation is to be done for at least twenty minutes. It is simple and yet not so easy as you will see.

Simplicity of heart means detachment from that which is not essential to our aim. It is the quest of reality and can only be accomplished with the open-heartedness of the child. You learn to look at the world with fresh eyes. The more your heart is emptied of opinions, beliefs, prejudices, and intellectual thoughts, the more abundantly the Light can shine into it.

7

Color, Crystals and Gemstones

The Spirit manifests color
Each vibratory ray
Calls forth from us
Its corresponding hue

Goethe, in his studies of color, discovered that light is the necessary basis of every color. They cannot exist without it. However, they are not light itself, but only modified light. He found that the element that causes this modification is darkness. Darkness to him was not the total and actionless absence of light; it was an activity. It sets itself in opposition to the light and enters into reciprocal action with it. He said light and darkness related to each other as the north and south poles of a magnet. Darkness can weaken the light in its action, and light can limit the energy of darkness. In each case, color arises. Light and darkness—the two cosmic polarities—are in continual interplay with all the objects existing in the visible world of space. In studying this primal phenomena in nature—color—we find universal laws.

Colors have been our friends for eternity. They gleam in the fire and play and sparkle in the waters.

Throughout all cultures, colors were chosen for their brilliance and harmonic qualities. We absorb color and light through our environment, our habitats, the clothes we wear, the beauty of nature, its flowers, fields and forests, the fruits and vegetables that nourish us. We can also absorb color through the application and wearing of crystals and gemstones.

Colors are necessary foods for our whole being, for our health and balance. We can heighten and refine our sensitivity to colors by deepening our appreciation for them. We can become more conscious of the relationship of their beauty and nature upon our hearts and souls. Nature speaks to us in colors and our senses are touched.

Communion with the soul of color lifts us beyond realms of matter, up into spheres of spirit and into cosmic space because light is universal and infinite.

The Rays

The rainbow — *l'arc-en-ciel* — is the purest possible manifestation of color. It reveals a wonderful mystery through the beauty and spiritual essence of the seven rays. In the spirits of the rays are centered all the potentialities of the highest dynamic powers and faculties. These are manifestations of qualities in life which, when understood, bring us to the whole totality of our being, as in the whole spectrum.

Arched high in the heavens, woven between sun and cloud, touching the depths, the earth, shining again and again its unequaled beauty and brilliance to mankind, the rainbow is a cosmic proclamation of the divinity inherent in each of us. It is a symbol of hope, faith, rejuvenation of

our inner creative capacities and regeneration of the sur-
roundings of our everyday life. It is our bridge between
the worlds.

Color Visualization

Let's begin with a simple color visualization. Sit comfort-
ably, touch your heart, feel the life pulse there. Then close
your eyes and imagine your heart as a center of pure,
white light radiating the rays of the rainbow. See a circular rainbow slowly filling your body. Feel these colors as
energies extending outward in every direction from the
center white light in your heart until you have become a
pulsing, radiant circular rainbow. Experience the peace
at the center of your heart. You may extend these colors
outside the body, into the aura. Consider the associations
that come to you. What emotions do you feel? What
colors did you most experience? Which colors didn't you
experience, or which seemed to be lacking?

Color Breathing

Problems connected with breathing are related to the
heart. The drawing in of the life breath, the sharing of air
with all other human beings relates to the right contact
with your environment. Breath is life force, vital force,
prana. Prana is that which underlies all physical action of
the body. It causes the circulation of the blood, the movement of the cells, in fact, all the motions upon which life
in the physical body depends. This vital force is in every

aspect of life. Prana is absorbed from food, water and of course the air you breathe. If you are afraid, or you experience a trauma of some sort, you don't breathe properly; very often you may almost stop breathing. Therefore I cannot stress enough the importance of deep rhythmic breathing. To magnify this energy, you want to combine it with color.

Color breathing techniques can provide you with understanding, power, beauty and health. You may simply visualize the life-giving radiance of the color you need, or you may take a stone of that color and put it in front of you. Breathe the color, breathe the stone deeply into you as you sit in a relaxed manner. Spend about ten to twelve minutes doing this, until you feel totally bathed and immersed in that ray.

White light is used for total protection and filling the heart and whole being with cosmic energy, health and peaceful vibrations. It increases and enlarges your perception and awareness. The heart opens to light, love and purity.

Green: As you know, the plant world is predominantly green, and there are many shades of it. Green stimulates a sense of balance, a connection to the earth. How do you experience yourself in nature? Green is invigorating and cheerful, generous and good-natured. It is the color of springtime, which means new-born life, hope and youth. It says "go ahead." It represents growth, creativity and faith. Feel the outpouring of healing and supply in your heart. Ask yourself: "Do you give your whole heart to whatever you do?"

Rose/Pink: When your heart is aching, when you feel alone or lonely, or perhaps you have lost a loved one, this is the color that will give you comfort and the realization that love is all around you. Feel and experience its tenderness, its gentleness, its softness. We are never alone! Touch a stone or look at a flower.

Green/Blue: Let yourself go to the freshness of water, perhaps to a lake or to the sea. Feel the coolness, the quieting, the tranquility. Experience the purity, power, beauty, and inspiration as your heart expands to the cosmos, to the infinite.

Golden Yellow: When you feel sad or depressed, imagine a ray of Sun coming into your heart bringing warmth, courage and wisdom. Golden yellow symbolizes the knowledge which overcomes ignorance, bringing wisdom and creativity like ripe corn. We all need to understand that all is energy, constantly changing and transforming. Experience the joy of life, the joy to live. The Sun's message is to be noble, large-hearted, optimistic and courageous.

Crystals and Gemstones

The stones that we are discussing in this book are significant entities. They are living, breathing, transmitting, interacting, shining, pulsating. They emit vibrations and frequencies which have very powerful effects on your heart and your whole being. They manifest light, life, colors, textures, vibrancy, transparency, clarity, or patterns which teach you about change. In times of transition, they aid in releasing old traumas, suppressed feelings and emotions, and old sufferings. The stones replace these with a sense of balance, stability, responsibility, a conscious intention of emotions, and the development of self-love and love through sharing.

Through the etheric body, the Earth is in constant communion with the Sun. The Earth patiently, but passionately, works on raw matter and extracts a sublime essence which is manifested in the healing stones: the crystal, diamond, emerald, sapphire, ruby, aquamarine, turquoise, tourmaline, and so on. From the celestial realms, the divine qualities and virtues have been reflected and materialized in a tangible, concrete way. The Earth offers these qualities as gifts to you to ennoble and spiritualize your heart.

The Earth's generosity and abundance toward all her children is boundless. It is equalled to the Sun who shines on everyone, regardless of good or bad, rich or poor, white, yellow, red or black. Only you need to open your heart to receive these gifts and feel gratitude in the very depth of your being.

Clear and White Stones
Crystal Quartz, Double-ended crystals, Herkimer diamonds, Moonstone and White Pearl

Crystal Quartz

Because of its clarity and transparency, the crystal is a symbol of radiant white light, of the ideal of soul attainment, the inner place of peace in the heart. It reflects the divine, and urges all human beings to be united in bonds of fellowship and love. In the crystal, matter overcomes itself, losing its original characteristic of opacity to become perfectly transparent.

The crystal quartz has the ability to balance, harmonize and bring equilibrium wherever it is used in the body or aura. It increases the awareness of light and ultimately makes you aware of any blocks.

In certain American Indian traditions, as well as in other cultures, the shaman or shamaness, during a ritual of initiation, would insert crystals in different parts of the body, but especially the heart of the initiate. This was not done physically, but ceremonially. It was a symbolic act to produce clarity and radiancy within.

To become the "Crystal in the Heart" means to embody and radiate the light and love of the sun to everyone alike, to become a bridge between the material and the spiritual.

Double-Ended Crystals

These are crystals that have perfected points on either end. They represent a balance: a balance between physical and spiritual, earthly and heavenly, or masculine and feminine polarities. They can be used on chakras but are especially useful as bridges between chakras. For example, you could lay a gold stone, such as amber or rutile quartz, on the solar plexus, then you would lay a double-ended crystal between the solar plexus and the heart center and a pink stone (such as rubellite) or green stone (such as chrysoprase) on the heart chakra. This would help make the connection between these two centers, would help release anxieties, and would bring strength, love and healing to the heart.

Herkimer Diamonds

These are crystals that have several perfected ends, sometimes three, four or five. They are clear and brilliant. Herkimer diamonds aid in integrating and harmonizing the different layers and aspects of the self. They also can be applied directly on a painful area. For example, I fell and hurt my knee badly some time ago. I taped a brilliant herkimer directly on my knee and also put one above and below my knee. This layout helped in letting the energies flow where they had been blocked by the fall.

Herkimers can also be worn on the throat or heart center to equalize these areas. They make beautiful jewelry!

Moonstone

The moonstone is connected to the moon, or the female aspect of your emotional nature. It cools, calms and soothes your reaction to emotional and personal situations. It is a great help to men who have had to suppress their emotions because of social codes which defined their behavior. The moonstone can help re-open and put these men in touch with their feminine, sensitive nature. This has only been a recent possibility for men. Since the popularizing of psychology and new age consciousness, men are beginning to realize that they feel, they have emotions, and they also have the right to express them.

As the sacred stone of India, the moonstone's message demonstrates that emotions are never to be suppressed, but need to be transformed into positive qualities. Many of the carvings on ancient temple doors were adorned with moonstones depicting male-female embraces. They symbolize the transcendence of personality through interpersonal fusion of male and female to reach union or overcome separateness.

A moonstone set in silver and worn as jewelry either on a chain against the heart (or as a ring) is extremely beneficial when you feel disconnected, out of touch from the Earth or from your own center.

Silver also represents the passive, receptive, mirror-like quality of the Moon which reflects the light of the Sun.

The White Pearl

This jewel of the sea fortifies and strengthens the heart. It has deep spiritual significance and brings you the message of transmutation. No matter how humble your beginnings are, you can attain the lustre and beauty of a pearl. You can attain a state of purity, peace and truth by shattering the emotional and mental patterns that have controlled you in the past.

The pearl teaches that life is experience — whether its deepest notes sound in joy or in tears. You cannot know your innermost Self without pain. In pain you resurrect and transmute. When you experience joy you build anew. The beautiful becomes even more beautiful. The richest heart is the one who has lived to the fullest. Thus within each of you lies the possibility of transformation and transmutation. The pearl can be re-energized by putting it in sea water for one night.

Green Stones
Emerald, Green Tourmaline, Malachite, Jade, Chrysoprase, Olivin-Peridot, Green Fluorite, Dioptase, Aventurin, Green Calcite

Emerald

The emerald is the goddess of gems. It has the capability to instill divine qualities through the power of its ray. It is a symbol of regeneration and life. The emerald is soothing and sympathetic, giving peace and harmony to the heart. It is both energizing and restful, replenishing and calming. It emits vibrations of balance, harmony, patience, and inspiration.

Its pure green spark bestows material and spiritual generosity to the heart and clears away feelings of avarice and envy. The emerald is a true symbol of the abundance and richness of the earth. Just by looking at it you'll feel restored and refreshed. I keep one on my desk and I look at it as I write, bathing myself in its brilliant, yet cool light. Its powerful clear ray magnetizes and amplifies, focuses and directs its light, much like a laser beam, transmuting illnesses and congestions of the heart.

The emerald represents new birth and the development of a revitalized and beautiful physical body in which the heart flowers (blooms) with creative and artistic abilities.

Green Tourmaline

The tourmaline is an unsurpassable stone, both in its benefits and in the beauty of its colors. It grows in columns, reminding us of the stalks of plants. It is a gem of translucent light and sometimes has layers and layers of color—shades of such subtle intensity—and if you are receptive, it will cast a spell of beauty, magic and fantasy on you. It is truly the wondrous stone of the New Age, bestowing joy and harmony in a full rainbow.

Its variety of green shades provide the balancing power of nature and the green ray of creativity and abundance of the earth. The green tourmaline is serene, restorative and healing. It has the potential to rejuvenate or regenerate the heart. Its electrical power is a great aid in shattering old concepts of self by urging you to begin anew on a higher level of consciousness. It heals illnesses of the heart, or problems with blood pressure and respiration, as in asthmatic conditions.

Malachite

Malachite is a symbol of change, of death and rebirth into a more creative life. The marvelous patterns of eyes, spirals, circles alternating with shaded bands teach you about change and flexibility. All is movement—your present life is a continuity of coming to be, passing away and immediate rebirth, like a flame that goes on burning but is never the same. There is continuity but not sameness.

Malachite is extremely healing for the heart. It helps release old programs or images of self so you can experience new levels of creativity.

The density and opaqueness in the malachite represent the physical, the material. Through the process of creating you come to understand the nature of spirit.

It was the sacred stone of Ancient Egypt, where it was used for its restorative and healing properties due to its high content of copper. Malachite has continually shown me how to let go of fixed ideas and embrace the new, the now.

Jade

Jade is the most respected stone in the Orient where it is a symbol of peace and tranquility. It has marvelous calming attributes. Jade constantly emits the healing vibration of harmony, bestowing the virtues of humility, wisdom, kindness, truth and courage.

The lighter shades are soothing to the nerves. The pale mauves and lilacs balance and calm the heart while raising consciousness. The shades of green (from light to imperial) are great healers to the emotionally troubled heart.

The jade has been known to bring good luck, inner strength and a long life.

Chrysoprase

This apple-green translucent gem is an excellent balancer for the emotions. It steadily emits a serene flow of light which has a sedative and tranquilizing effect on the heart. Especially it is very effective in soothing heart palpitations.

The chrysoprase seems to have the ability to clarify, bringing unconscious thoughts up to a conscious level. It also strengthens inner vision by bringing a sense of harmony, understanding, and purpose to the wearer.

Peridot or Olivin

Because of its golden green, soft glow, the peridot raises the consciousness from the solar plexus area into the heart. It has a very cleansing and purifying influence, supplying balance and tranquility to the emotions.

The peridot brings golden warmth and relieves the heart of melancholia, replacing it with inspiration and wisdom.

Green Fluorite

The fluorite grows into cubic forms in different shades of exquisite green crystals from pale to more vibrant hues. Its message states that wisdom comes from harmony, that harmony comes from contemplation, that contemplation comes from peace and that inner peace leads to inner gladness and inner light.

It also is a great help in grounding excess energies and helps you operate at optimum efficiency, even while handling tremendous amounts of frequencies in your physical body, thus aiding in keeping your emotions centered.

Dioptase

The dioptase, with its beautiful deep green bewitching crystals, is still young and evolving into the vibrational potency of emeralds. Its strong green light, eternally new with the abundance of the earth, charges the heart with the power of universal healing and supply.

Aventurine

The aventurine is a fairly translucent quartz with a little glitter. It is a humble stone which brings you to a greater awareness of nature and plants. Its influence is quieting and tranquilizing and can be used either as a touchstone to lay on the heart, or just to have around you.

A large aventurine was passed from hand to hand at the Offering Ceremony during the Conference on Healing with Crystals and Gemstones. It received the energy of everyone in the gathering and was returned to the Earth as a loving prayer, side by side with the great crystal.

Green Calcite

Green calcite is a lovely pale shade of green which has proven to me lately to be extremely healing and quieting to the heart. It exerts a peaceful and serene influence during the process of dissolving old patterns and blocks, especially old fears.

Pink Stones
Ruby, Rubellite, Watermelon Tourmaline, Kunzite, Rhodochrosite, Rhodonite, Rose Quartz and copper metal

Ruby

The ruby, although it is considered red, is truly a stone of the heart. It sparkles with the light, fire, warmth and intensity of the Sun. From clear red to different shades of pink, it teaches that love must be lifted toward the light of universal love, toward compassion for all life. Compassion consents to experience the trials of human suffering in order to better transmute them. It is pure love. Love is essentially pure reason and not an emotional sentiment expressing itself through kind actions. The ruby symbolizes the heart of spiritual love and devotion through purification and transfiguration.

The light in the heart illuminates the whole being as in the Illuminati. The ruby bestows positive life qualities such as courage, fearlessness and strength. It activates and vitalizes the circulation, thus heating and stimulating the heart and body.

Honor and value this gem for its life- and love-giving qualities, for compassion and universal love are so needed throughout this beautiful and wondrous planet Earth.

$$\bullet \quad \bullet \quad \bullet$$

A friend of mine told me the following story, which he said come from an old Sufi legend.

A long time ago, a Caliph forbade singing. When a dervish heard this, his heart contracted into a lump and he became very ill. No one could find the cause of his sickness. He finally died. The doctor, who had been treating him, was curious to find the cause of his death. He opened his body and found a big lump red as ruby where the heart should be. As the doctor needed money, he sold the precious stone. After going through different owners, it finally ended up in the hands of the Caliph, who had it set into a ring.

One day, while wearing the ruby ring, the Caliph started to sing. All at once, his clothes turned red, his ruby was boiling like hot oil and flowing all over his clothes like blood. Wishing to understand the mysterious secret of the ruby, he called on all his subjects to find all of its previous owners. Finally, he was told by the doctor the sad story of the singing dervish.

Rubellite or Pink Tourmaline

The rubellite comes in a solid color variety from deep red or pink to almost violet shades. Its mission is to lead from the heart, strengthening the will to love and to sacrifice. It symbolizes the purity of maternal love.

This precious gem's warm hue helps you open your heart to yourself, to perceive your own self-worth, your own beauty and your own divinity. Love begins with trusting yourself, for inside you all have the power to accomplish all things.

Rubellite resembles the ruby in directing, channeling and intensifying devotional urges and impulses, thus promoting love for humanity. By giving insight and perception to emotions, it removes conflict and pain that have led you to dispair and grief, adding tenderness to your heart.

The rubellite brings the realization that the love exists in every aspect of life, thus bringing you to unity.

Never fail, whatever may befall you,
be it good or evil, to keep your heart
quiet and calm in the tenderness of love.
St. John of the Cross

The Watermelon Tourmaline

The watermelon tourmaline is a bi-colored gem with fascinating qualities. When cross sections are cut, it looks like a slice of watermelon because of its green rind and pink core. It symbolizes the pair of opposites, the principles of yin-yang. Therefore it can balance and redirect imbalances and guilt produced by conflicts and confusion. The message of the watermelon tourmaline is to be self-contained, integrated, secure and in harmony with the different aspects of self.

The green feeds the life-force, healing and harmonizing the heart, while the pink soothes, calms and brings affection and tenderness.

Kunzite

In a dream I heard a voice telling me to go find some kunzite when I didn't even know of its existence or how to spell it. So I did. Its message was very clear: "It is the flow of energy from the heart of the human being to the heart of the source that heals, rejuvenates, strengthens and expands your being."

Kunzite grows with a striated structure, resembling the tourmaline, which means that the electrical impulses run through the length of the crystal. It ranges from light pink to deeper shades of lilac on its edges, which symbolizes that pain and old sufferings are to be transmuted to spiritual awareness and understanding. In other words, the emotions of the heart need to be experienced consciously, in order to be raised to a higher level of spirit. You can let go of your personal sufferings and face the infinite love of spirit.

This wondrous stone acts like a sword of light and truth. It removes pain within the heart with a sword-like energy. For me it has become an invaluable tool in healing the heart.

Rhodochrosite

Rhodochrosite comes in a variety of forms and shades from translucent golden red crystals to opaque soft shades of pink with white swirls and patterns. This gem is a great help in your development. The goal of all development is integration — integration as a personality, integration in the heart, integration in the whole.

The radiant golden red crystals teach you love of life, love of unity, love of love. As we all come to this understanding and become conscious of this truth, peace will be present in every heart. Look at a person in love, doesn't he or she look younger, more alive, vibrant? There is a glow about love. Remember to try to express your life more lovingly.

The pink tones will teach you of the mingling of human love with the white purity of aspiration, as well as of human affection that has been softened by sorrow. These stones soothe the heart, arouse tender feelings of love, softness and compassion.

Rhodonite

The rhodonite ranges from light to darker shades of pink, laced with black veins. The black in the stone symbolizes the unconscious, the hidden, while the pink represents love and affection.

The stone brings out unrest from the depths of the heart. It brings up confusion and conflicts. By making you aware and conscious of these, it promotes understanding and acceptance of the self.

Rose Quartz

The rose quartz is the most humble of all the pink stones and yet is unequaled in its qualities of softness, tenderness, affection and love. It promotes feelings of self love and then radiates them into unselfish and constant affection toward others. Aggressive, hostile or anxiety-ridden behavior can be tranquilized by the potent yet gentle effects of pink-rose quartz.

These stones are favorites of little girls and elderly women alike as we all need to reawaken and remember the gentleness in our hearts.

In gentleness there is great strength.
Power most of the time can be
a very quiet thing.
                              Sun Bear

Copper metal

Copper has a warm pink glow which speaks of the attributes of the goddess Venus. Those qualities are love, friendliness, beauty, harmony and a deep appreciation for all the creative arts, such as music, dance, literature, painting and healing.

This is a great metal to utilize in combination with gold and with all pink and red stones. There are traces of copper in turquoise, chrysocolla, malachite and azurite which add a healing and calming vibration to these stones.

Blue/Green Stones
Aquamarine, Turquoise, Chrysocolla, Amazonite

Aquamarine

The aquamarine, a transparent luminous stone, is the stone of mystics and pure-hearted seers who feel everything. The green-blue of the cosmic sea reflects the light effects of the sun on waves. It teaches you that love releases, love adjusts and interprets, and love heals on all planes.

Its effect is subtle and soft, yet long-lasting in stabilizing the emotional blocks in the heart and throat. How much have you swallowed? Because of this, so often, you are unable to express your true feelings in the present. The aquamarine helps you retain purity and innocence while helping you achieve clarity of vision.

> Man at his best, like water . . .
> Loves living close to the earth
> Living clear down in his heart.
> Lao Tse

Turquoise

The turquoise is a symbol of the sea, which speaks of the depth of the soul, and of the sky which shows you infinity in the limitless heights of ascension. Opaque as the Earth, yet it lifts your spirit, bringing wisdom. It is old, yet young.

> The wisdom that was not made,
> but is at this present as it hath ever been,
> and so shall ever be.
> St. Augustine

To the Egyptian, Persian, Tibetan Buddhist, American Indian and Gypsy, this stone has been a symbol of purity, spirit, life and breath — a guardian of the Earth and of the body, heart and soul.

In American Indian culture as well as in the Gypsy culture, it is used for healing practically everything. Because of its high copper content (as in the malachite and chrysocolla) this healing influence is magnified and very beneficial, for it removes congestions and blocks in the chest, heart and throat area.

Chrysocolla

The chrysocolla is the younger sister of the turquoise, but it carries more light and is sometimes very translucent. A stone of Venus, it is a symbol of beauty, love and harmony. It is gentle yet powerful. It reminds me of the quality of humility which promotes listening and looking with the heart.

Its calming influence helps to alleviate fears and guilt that prevents you from relaxing. It restores peace and harmony to the heart.

Amazonite

The amazonite, the most humble of the blue-green stones, is opaque like the turquoise, but sometimes has crystallized veins. It teaches that pain can be alleviated through consciousness and creativity. Its luminous color bestows calmness and tranquility to the heart by purifying cloudy feelings and emotions.

Golden/Yellow Stones
Rutile Quartz, Topaz, Amber, Citrine,
Golden Fluorite, Apatite and gold metal

Rutile Quartz

This clear crystal contains inclusions of rutile fibers of golden and reddish color which are highly valuable. These fibers bear cross-currents of electrical charges that amplify healing by bringing heat, warmth and balance to congested areas of the heart. Sometimes they make beautiful patterns and symbols which hold magnetic force fields.

The golden ray has the ability to bring in the power of the sun. It dissolves disturbances, fear, anxiety, and sadness in the heart, replacing these attitudes with strength and courage.

The rutile quartz has become a favorite stone for many of my clients, who hold it in their hands when needing to be fearless in personal situations or confrontations.

Golden Topaz

The topaz has an inspiring and stimulating influence on the heart and soul. Its golden light reminds me of the halo that very often comes out of the hearts of saints and spreads out to their auras. It lifts above the mundane, the mediocre, and soars up into infinity, reaching toward the Light.

Its electrifying nature magnetizes your whole being which means that your heart is charged with greater capacity, bringing awareness, keenness, clarity, and concentration. This strong influence has a balancing effect in cases where emotional traumas weigh heavy. The topaz is a symbol of the Sun's radiating nature, bringing illumination to darkness through the power of love.

Amber

The amber is a light-weight gem. Its origin is organic vegetable matter that was composed of various saps. These mineralized and fossilized, sometimes retaining organic inclusions such as insects, ferns and flowers, which give positive additional energies. This wonderful uninterrupted flow of life is a proclamation of the power of nature.

Its strong magnetic flow balances and stabilizes the heart. Heart ailments of all kinds, from slight irregularity in beat caused by nervous indigestion, to more serious problems, respond favorably to the pure deep golden ray of the Sun in the amber.

Citrine Quartz

Through its golden color, the citrine bears the signature of wisdom and peace. Most of the citrine available today is amethyst — violet quartz — which has been baked and therefore turned into a golden yellow. This process resembles a natural process in the earth, using the power of fire and heat to transform. The citrine removes thought forms that block energy moving up from the solar plexus to the heart. It aids in transmuting emotional fears. Its healing influence is of great value against depression.

Golden Fluorite

The fluorite also grows in golden shades which sometimes are intermingled with bands or areas of violet. These colors are a direct stimulant to the heart and aid in developing intuition. Its golden transparency has the ability to open your heart to cosmic consciousness and wisdom.

Apatite

The apatite is a lovely golden-green crystal which captures rainbows and brings warmth and healing to the sorrows or insecure feelings of the heart. It is a more humble stone than its sister, the topaz, but emits radiating qualities and vibrations of harmony and balance.

Gold

Gold symbolizes the perfection of the mineral realm in which complementary ingredients are indissolubly combined. It means the cessation of antagonism and the reaching of perfection. Gold is a great conductor of the life-giving energy of the Sun, bestowing its radiant qualities of warmth, strength, courage, generosity, self-confidence and awareness. The person who has a "heart of gold" is someone who carries the finest of these qualities: giving of himself, being generous, warm, and loving.

The healing properties of gold are extremely beneficial to anyone who is experiencing sadness or depression. You may wear gold, or rub gold on your heart, or even drink "gold water" (water in which gold has been dipped).

Gold is the ultimate state of transmutation, the end-product associated with alchemy, compared to the philosopher's stone which has miraculous powers of divination and healing.

Laying the Stones on the Heart Chakra

There are several ways to use stones or crystals to release old traumas and sufferings from the heart. You may begin by putting one stone on the heart center. You may then wish to progress to different lay-outs. Proceed slowly and trust your inner voice. Before you begin, remember to take time to relax your body by doing some deep breathing, some stretching, and perhaps some yoga postures.

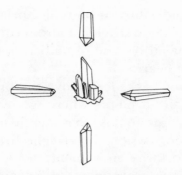

Figure 10. The Cross pattern. This pattern releases old traumas and sufferings. Place a cluster crystal on the heart center, surrounded by four single crystals.

Wear a natural fiber undershirt of white or neutral shade. Remove all stones after fifteen to twenty minutes.

Crystals

Using only clear crystals, you may put a cluster, which is a crystal that has several smaller ones within it, on the heart center and then lay four single crystals around it. The points of the single crystals should point to the center crystal, in a cross pattern, as shown in figure 10.

Clear quartz crystals are excellent for absorbing negativity and they perform the unique service of removing it from the heart. They also aid in balancing and decongesting blocks in the heart.

Crystal Heart Massage

To remove old blocks, pains and knots in the heart, a simple and tender method is to give a heart massage with a fairly small, but clear and perfect-ended crystal. You may do it on yourself, or better yet have a friend or loved one give it to you. I have found that it is preferable to wear a light undershirt of natural fabric such as silk or cotton, white or neutral color. I also recommend that you light incense or oil or rose of amber as these scents are soothing to the heart.

Lie on your back, feel above the breasts for knots. We all have painful points where we hide our pain. In these points you are to poke very gently and then rub the crystal away, on its side. Follow the breast all around, under, in a clockwise movement, tenderly, giving love and affection as you encounter areas of old pain. Spend at least ten to fifteen minutes on each breast. You may want to rinse the crystal in sea-salt water during the procedure, especially if you feel it has absorbed negativity, or when there has been much trauma in the heart. Finish by lying the crystal on the heart center with the apex (or point) facing up for a few more minutes. Through its electrical power the crystal will aid in dissolving the pain. Try to keep aware of the pictures, images, or feelings that arise. Ask yourself, "What is their message?" Allow yourself to let go and forgive.

Only Green Stones

Malachite, jade, tourmaline, chrysoprase, aventurine. You may use any of these stones in combination, or you may prefer to use only one kind of stone. Trust yourself. These stones are all nourishing and harmonizing. You can put a larger green stone of your choice on the heart center, which is a little hollow center between the breasts. Then you can add other green stones and create beautiful patterns. For example, you could make a cross pattern by putting a malachite in the center, and four aventurines top, bottom and to either side of it. Make any pattern that your intuition guides you to create!

Figure 11. This positioning helps to open an emotionally constricted throat.

Only Blue/Green Stones

Use a combination of turquoise, chrysocolla and aquamarine, moving from the heart center up toward the throat. These beauteous shades of the sea and sky lift your heart toward inspiration and beauty. On the physical level, these stones are wonderful for decongesting blocked areas of the heart and throat. They are also used for cooling and calming when the heart is excited.

Here is a layout I recommend to help open the throat from emotions tied. Put one chrysocolla on the heart center, and two pieces of turquoise, laid horizontally, above it, and then one aquamarine on the throat center (see figure 11).

Figure 12. The Spiral pattern. To be used with green and pink stones laid clockwise over the heart. Combines the nourishing life force with warmth and tenderness.

Pink and Green Stones

These can be combined to form a clockwise spiral on the heart. (See figure 12.) These complement and supplement each other — the green nourishing life force with the warmth and tenderness of pink, for example rose quartz and green chrysoprase.

Only Pink Stones

Rubellite, rose quartz, kunzite, rhodochrosite and rhodonite can be used to relieve pain and sorrow. You may wish to put one in the center and four around it. I also recommend that the client hold small clear crystals in his or her hands.

Only Gold Stones

Citrine, topaz, rutile quartz, golden fluorite, amber. Use these when the heart is weak and tired, or if the individual is very sensitive and gets hurt easily. He or she needs the strength of the Sun, the warmth and energy of the golden ray. It is also good to wear a gold chain, for example on the chest and heart area.

Combination of Green, Blue-Green, Pink and Gold Stones

These can be used on the heart area for healing, quieting, giving love, affection and courage.

As you work deeply on the heart, you may wish to balance some of the other centers by adding stones that are not mentioned as heart stones. For example, sometimes it is necessary to put stones like black tourmaline and/or red jasper — which are very good at grounding energies — on the first chakra; orange carnelian on the second chakra for earth energy; and gold stones on the solar plexus for strength. You can also use a clear crystal on the third eye to help clear your vision. The apex or point of the crystal should always be facing up. Hold clear crystals in your hands to help comfort you.

. . .

I would like to share what happened in one of my groups: During a balancing chakra layout, a man quite heavy in his body had put one stone of each color on his centers and a rose quartz on his heart. As he shared his experience he said:

"I saw little spirits going in and out of the stones, then the chief, the leader appeared and told them all to leave, that he was taking over. The chief then looked at all the stones chosen and found them satisfactory. Then he told me that the humble rose quartz was quite adequate but that in future times I should look for a crystallized rose quartz. He continued to say that the crystallized rose quartz was very powerful in allowing love to move more freely in the heart."

What a great experience! I personally took the chief's advice and must admit that he was right. Although a crystallized rose quartz is more expensive because of its rarity, it is truly a flower for the heart — to soften and expand the love.

8

Shared Experiences

Going beyond all likes and dislikes
See each thing in its perfection
A stone, a flower, a person, a star
Each a world in itself
And all connected to All

In the workshops that I have given over the last few years, I have come to realize how much we all need to let go of past sufferings and fears in order to progress on our spiritual path. By breaking down the confines of the personality, we can experience immense elation and freedom which leads us to a higher consciousness, a feeling of communality with everyone, a sensation of world harmony. I have witnessed beautiful transformations in people when the blocks and knots of the heart are dissolved and the joy comes in.

As I begin a group or individual session, I always work in a ceremonial way. I begin by setting up an altar to the four elements: a candle for fire, a bowl of water, feathers and incense for air, and a stone, rock and crystal for earth. I always include a humble rock to remind myself and others of our humble beginnings. This ritual has developed over many years and comes from my understanding and respect for the elements and the source. I walk around the room praying to the Great Spirit and call on the protection of the White Light. I then chant/sing to the stones as I uncover them and bring them out of their cloth. During this ceremony, which is an inner preparation, I enter into harmony. Something is released and I come in tune, in communion with the cosmic creative forces. I have also realized that I reach a state of impersonality that allows me to feel deeply with the people who are going through experiences of suffering and old pains without being swayed by them. It has taken me years to get to this point, but I can now empathize and participate without being torn apart by the energy.

Very often after doing some breathing techniques and movements, I like to laugh with groups that I work with. We do the laughing Buddha exercise, which means we all start laughing together — we laugh and laugh and laugh, releasing our own seriousness and letting go of tensions through laughter, thus freeing the heart. Sometimes some people just can't. They feel foolish, self-conscious, then they become defensive and there it is, so clearly: we get so attached to our self-important images that we cannot switch and become clowns even for a little while. Try it sometime! Laugh until you are rolling on the floor — it feels so good. Laughing at ourselves is of prime importance, laughing at the situation or circumstances we have created enables us to take a step back and observe ourselves. Making faces is also another favorite relaxation technique for me.

We also work in groups with the voice — making sounds, chanting. Very often I chant as the people are lying down with the stones on their chakras. Syllables come to me, chants unknown to me, chants of the Earth, as if the Earth wants to express herself not only through stones but also through sound and songs. Many people have experienced this as the voice of the Earth soothing them, comforting them or sending them into other worlds, other spheres and putting a protective field around them.

Experiences

A young man came to visit me. His manner was timid and awkward. I felt that his heart was open and sensitive but that he needed more strength and self-confidence. I laid some red jasper for grounding and carnelian for earth energy on his first and second chakras, rutilated quartz on his solar plexus, green and pink tourmalines on his heart and aquamarines on his throat. After a deep silent time he said, "I felt a strong flow of power coming from the heart of the Earth. It felt like a lightning bolt! It entered my heart and I had the impression that the Earth had accepted me totally." He was beaming. This young man had actually experienced his connection with his greater mother and was a transformed person. He felt strong, self-assured and in unity and peace with himself.

. . .

A woman who had never felt herself beautiful chose a gold topaz to put on her throat. This is the image that came to her: She saw a gold dust falling upon her and transforming her into a golden radiating beauty. For the first time in her life, through this blessing, she perceived herself linked to the Sun, to the source of light. Her heart was exalted with this divine realization.

. . .

An elderly woman, who had repressed many of her own wishes and feelings for the "good" of the family, had this experience after putting a rhodochrosite on her heart: She saw a radiant and beautiful flower unfolding in her heart. She experienced a state of grace — a rebirth — a new life was taking place. She knew that she was to live her life consciously, without any guilt or worries, in freedom and love.

. . .

A middle-aged man, unsure of his life, his work, his goals, came to a session. He needed grounding and needed to believe in his creativity. I laid some black tourmaline and some red jasper on the first chakra, some citrine at the navel point, and four green stones — chrysoprase, malachite, aventurine, and green tourmaline — around an emerald on the heart center. He saw and felt a tree rooted deep in his heart, roots also going all the way down to his feet into the Earth. The tree was tall and strong with branches radiating out, some even bearing fruits. This image was so important to this man, it impressed his imagination so strongly, that he knew it would only be a short time before he would realize it. He knew that he was the tree, tall and strong, rooted in the Earth, reaching out to the heavens, bearing fruit — creativity.

. . .

A woman artist/painter came into a group totally blocked, closed off. She was late and actually wanted to leave but finally decided to stay and to go through the course. During one of the layouts, she chose a moonstone to put on her throat. As she relaxed and allowed the messages to come in, something tight in her was released and she heard a voice say to her that she was to paint each ray of the rainbow one at a time in its different hues in order to absorb their qualities. She saw the colors. She was not to concern herself with forms. It was such a clear and straight message. She felt incredible joy that she could begin painting again and heal herself through her creativity. In a previous session, we had worked with the image of her father, who she said was "a real painter." Of course, by saying this she was measuring herself against him, feeling unworthy. Because she did not run away, she came in contact with her own source of beauty and creativity and could begin her own healing process — by letting go of old images of inferiority.

● ● ●

Of course, there are many times when people experience images of deep suffering. As we work on the heart, old memories arise. Remember that memories are locked in the heart.

One woman experienced her heart being cut and offered as a sacrifice to the gods. She saw herself being placed on an altar and a knife being driven through her heart. This image released some blocks that had prevented her from accepting her life. She also came to realize that by having gone through this suffering she had been purified and could now have compassion in her heart. She came to understand that through death there is rebirth, thus a continuing movement toward transformation and transfiguration.

Women, especially as they go back to past memories, sometimes remember themselves as witches and experience guilt. As they let go of moral judgments in their hearts — of good and evil, condemnation and blame — they are freed to begin forgiving themselves, to forgive others, and to recognize that in the unity of light and darkness there arises the sacred flame of the enlightened heart.

. . .

As we work with the heart, we discover that the solar plexus (below the heart) and the throat (above the heart) are two very sensitive centers that can prevent the heart from being open and whole by blocking the flow of energy. Thus it is important that as we lay pink and green stones on the heart center we also put gold stones on the solar plexus and blue-green stones on the throat. Here are some examples:

In one of my workshops there was a man who I felt was truly on the path of the heart. He was warm and generous, yet he said to me, "I can't stand to look at this turquoise; it seems like poison to me." It was hard to believe what he said as he pointed to a beautiful blue-green piece. So during the next layout of stones, I asked him to pick one. At first he couldn't. His resistance was high, so I pushed him gently and he finally did. On his heart I put a rose quartz and pink and green tourmalines, an amber on his navel point, the turquoise that he didn't like on his throat and I gave him some crystals to hold on his hands. After a few minutes, he began shaking, convulsing and crying. I went to him, touched him on the heart and forehead and waited. Afterward he shared his experience. He had returned to a time in his childhood when he felt a great deal of loneliness and sadness. All these years he had hidden these feelings from himself and had not allowed himself to express his pain. His dislike for all blue-green color was a key, an opening. As we worked together, he allowed himself to express and release and finally to accept this color, symbol of opening of the throat, in himself and his life.

Another man displayed his discomfort with a golden stone, a golden fluorite. He was a gentle being. The stone's message to him was that he was to take the power of the Sun unto himself. He was to acknowledge and take his power. There was to be no more confusion between gentleness and strength. All of us need to be empowered in ourselves even though we are gentle, otherwise we become weak or meek in our hearts.

Perhaps we have misused power in the past and unconscious memories prevent us from taking our power in the present. So let us clear these old blocks and remember that even the most compassionate heart needs to be courageous and strong. The heart is a rock upon which strongholds can be built.

. . .

Another important thing I have realized is that we all choose colors and stones that we like or feel comfortable with and we rarely question ourselves as to why we do not like a particular stone or color. So, sometimes in group or individual work, I ask the people to choose something they don't like. Sometimes the reaction is so strong that people feel repulsion at this.

The missing piece! What is missing in you? This is a clue to knowing yourself better. What is your missing link? Each of you will experience it in a different way. Yet it is this missing piece that prevents you from feeling whole, integrated in your heart. The deeper you go into your unconsciousness, the more you will realize that you carry pictures or patterns that need healing. The heart is the center of your being — the center of your universe. The whole universe is in your heart! Here are some examples of these experiences:

Two highly developed and spiritual women came together to a group. I sensed in them a lack of touch with the earth, also a lack of communal sharing. I asked them to choose stones and/or colors they didn't like or feel connected to. One woman chose a red coral; the other a dark reddish-brown jasper. The results were amazing. The red coral spoke to the woman of vitality, life-essence, that she (the woman) was not to push away this color because she would be pushing away life itself. She was told that she needed this color for strength and courage to meet daily experiences and also that life was to be connected with the heart. In other words, she was to love and respect the heart because the source of life infuses all life forms.

The other woman had difficulty being in and accepting her body. She told me that in the last years she had put on a lot of weight. In her case, the stone — jasper — grounded her. She felt the earth and her body but as she spoke she couldn't bear to look at it as she thought it was so ugly. I asked her to put it in front of her and understand the message. She realized that she was speaking of her own body. She felt her body to be ugly. She wanted to hide it. The stone told her that she had to make peace with her own "earth" (body).

To be integrated in your heart means that you are to regard your own form filled with spirit and light as a temple. How can you love outside yourself when you do not respect your own Earth? Or how can you feel yourself to be "spiritual" and not respect the house of your spirit?

Another woman chose a dark grayish stone. In her visual journey, she was led to a tunnel. At the end of the tunnel there was fog. She sensed light, but couldn't enter into it yet. Then a voice said, "You are just like me; you are not letting your colors show. You are hiding behind this grayness." Here again the message was so clear. The woman wept and said, "It's true, it's true. I don't show myself, I don't show my colors. I'm afraid." As you awake in your heart and are willing to face yourself, you become a warrior—your heart is open and raw facing the unknown—life.

Very often, people experience the image of armor on the heart. Yes, perhaps it was necessary for a while to protect your heart, but you must let the armor melt gently. No need to pull it off sharply. The more you trust in life and that life is the activity of the universe impelled by love, the more you will come in touch with your spiritual heart.

What is the Spiritual Heart?

Sometimes people ask me, "How do you know that a chakra is blocked?" I answer that I don't know. As I work with a person, I sense something and then I follow my intuition. I cannot describe it or teach it. It just happens. Through all the work I have done, I have learned that we are all mirrors for each other. Thus in a group when one experiences a pain, a block, or an attachment, it usually sparks off something in someone else. Humanity is humanity—the sharing that takes place in the groups is a lesson for each one of us—including myself. I see my pain in others. I see their pain in myself. Sometimes as I share my own experiences people see that they, too, can overcome a problem.

Let me share now a personal pain. As a child I stuttered. It was embarrassing and painful. I had chosen a mother who spoke for me and for everyone in the family. This period passed but it was always very difficult for me to express myself. Then I married very young, had two children and within a few years the stuttering returned, but this time even stronger. I became so bad that I couldn't say my own name, I couldn't answer a telephone, I just wanted to hide. Yes, you have guessed it. My husband had taken over the role of my mother. I sought help and I remember so clearly the psychologist saying to me, "You cannot say your name because you do not know who you are. You are playing the roles and images that people have of you." I knew I had to leave my old life, my environment. It took me years of hard work to let go of the fear of speaking and, of course, to forgive. But I have overcome it. I had to go very deep inside and acknowledge my own self—I had to accept myself and love myself. Now I stand in front of hundreds of people sometimes when I give lectures and I even sing—you can too!

I also like to work with movement, dance, the body. The body never lies. Tom Ehrlich, my companion, and I often work with groups together. His tool is the drum — the heart beat. As we come into the rhythm of the heart beat within the movement of the body, something clicks. Sometimes it is a gentle, quiet movement and sometimes people go into wild dances, gestures. Through them something is released. Then often there is surrender. Sometimes people need to fall, collapse, and come again. Sometimes the body expresses a prayer to the greater heart.

Thus through silence, sound, movement, the laying on of stones, we come to understand that we live in many realities simultaneously and we need to give expression to the different aspects of our being in order to be more integrated and whole. When we forget our connectedness and we become sad, let us also accept these times. Let us be grateful for all experiences. We are to remember that on the path of the heart, there is no escapism, there are no excuses. We welcome the shocks that come to disturb us in order to push us into the changes that need to take place.

The healing and opening of the heart means that we have accepted ourselves, made peace and come to love the Earth. We have let go of past suffering, our attachments to pain. We live in the now. We trust in not knowing where we are going. We have faith. We have forgiven ourselves and others. We see light and darkness as qualities merging and dancing into Oneness — the Sacred Marriage. We are open, like a lotus to life, love, beauty, spirit. There is spontaneity, joy, contentment and grace.

We experience the power and fullness, the gentleness of our spiritual heart! The spiritual heart is the center of spiritual fire, source of intelligence of the heart, spiritual source of light and love. The symbol of harmony, sympathy, creativity, health and courage. The place of truth and love; the place of beauty.

Touch your heart and remember in gratitude and in love.

Conclusion

When you fix your heart on one point
then nothing is impossible for you.
— *Buddha*

The awesomeness of the heart is staggering to all cultures who use symbols as the language by which nature speaks. The whole universe lives in our hearts: the Sun, Moon, stars, oceans, rivers, lakes, woods, trees, flowers, stones, good people, bad people, heavens and hells. Myriads of things are within the heart, within our nature.

The goal is to be reborn in the heart with the essence of quality, beauty, generosity, all giving, all knowing from deep within. All that we seek for is within the heart, within each one of us once the battle, the transformation and the re-integration has taken place. Let us remember that each day we all are born and die anew. Each day we experience the sunrise and sunset.

At this present period, the vision of the Golden Age is asking for the wholeness of human personality, a totality of life in which we acknowledge the false separation between us and nature and move toward a unity and a communion with the universe. We need to acknowledge the sacredness in each human being—the equality, dignity, integrity and the potential for self-realization in the heart of each person. Once the Ego and the impersonal Self have merged there can be only a fusion, an intensity of life in which all is joy and gratefulness. Each one of us is a beautiful flower which simply needs to open to receive all it needs. To live in the "awakened heart" means to live a life of love, of freedom and peace, to meet the destiny that has inspired mystics, poets, artists, scientists and to perceive the treasure house of beauty within the Heart of hearts.

• • •

An old Hindu legend tells that once upon a time all men and women were gods and goddesses. But they abused their divinity so much that Brahma, the master of the gods, decided to remove their divine power and hide it in a place where it would be impossible for them to find. The great problem was to find a suitable hiding place.

When the minor gods were summoned to a council to resolve the problem, they proposed this: "Let us bury the divinity of human beings in the earth." But Brahma responded: "No, this doesn't suffice, because they will dig and find it."

Then the gods replied: "In this case let us throw the divinity in the deepest of the oceans."

But Brahma answered again: "No, because sooner or later, people will explore the depths of all oceans and it is certain that one day they will find it and will bring it to the surface."

Then the minor gods concluded: "We do not know where to hide it because there doesn't seem to exist on earth or in the sea a place where people cannot reach one day."

Then Brahma said: "Here is what we will do with the divinity of the human being: we will hide it in the deepest part of themselves, because that is the only place where they will never think to look for it."

From that time on, concludes the legend, human beings have been around the world, they have explored, climbed, dived and dug, in search of something that is within.

A Prayer

Heart

O my heart
beat gently upon my breast —
in rhythm with the heart of earth —
with joy and gratitude
to the Greater Heart.
Love,
Life,
Beauty and
Freedom are
One.

Stones for the Heart Relationship of Ray, Chakra and Color

Table 1. Stones for the Heart

White Stones	Purity and Balance
Crystal Quartz	Balances, harmonizes, increases awareness, aids in producing clarity and radiance.
Double-ended Crystal	Represents balance in polarities; to be used as a bridge between centers.
Herkimer Diamond	Clear, brilliant, with several perfected ends; aids in integrating and harmonizing different aspects of the self.
Moonstone	Cooling, calming, soothing to emotions—good for men and women.
Pearl	Fortifies and strengthens, transmutes, shatters controlling emotional and mental patterns.
Silver Metal	Passive, receptive, good for white and blue stones.

Table 1. Continued

Green Stones	Healing and Harmonizing
Emerald	Divine qualities, regeneration, soothing, and sympathetic, brings peace and harmony. Both energizing and restful, replenishing and calming, brings patience, balance, inspiration, creativity, generosity. Symbol of abundance of earth.
Green Tourmaline	Balancing, serene, restorative, healing, rejuvenates, regenerates, shatters old concepts — also creative.
Malachite	Change, death and rebirth. Teaches all life is movement, let go and release, pushes creativity.
Jade	Harmony, humility, patience, wisdom, kindness, heals troubled heart.
Chrysoprase	Balances, sedates, tranquilizes, soothes heart palpitations. Has ability to clarify problems, brings harmony and understanding.
Peridot or Olivin	Relieves heart of melancholia. Connects to solar force, replaces with inspiration and wisdom.

Table 1. Continued

Green Fluorite	Harmony, inner gladness.
Dioptase	Healing and universal supply.
Aventurine	Quieting, tranquilizing.
Green Calcite	Dissolves blocks—especially old fears—calming.
Pink Stones	Soothing and Love Oriented
Ruby	Love towards universality, compassion for all life, devotion, through flame of purification brings courage, fearlessness, strength.
Rubellite (Pink Tourmaline)	Opens heart to your Self, your beauty and individuality, brings trust that promotes love for humanity, pure love.
Watermelon Tourmaline	Pair of opposites—green is healing, life force energy; pink soothes, calms and brings affection. Balances and redirects guilt from confusion and conflict, promotes security, integration, self-containment.

Table 1. Continued

Kunzite	Helps to transmute old pains into spiritual awareness and understanding. Helps to let go of sufferings and face love.
Rhodochrosite	Helps to integrate personality, heart, spirit, and love of life.
Rhodomite	Brings up unconscious conflicts, unrest, confusion, promotes understanding and acceptance of the self.
Rose Quartz (Humble and Crystallized)	Softness, tenderness, affection, love. Great for tranquilizing aggressive, hostile behavior. Promotes self-love and then radiates it to others.
Copper Metal	Good for all pink and gold stones. Symbol of Venus, warm and balancing.
Blue/Green Stones	Calming and Tranquilizing
Aquamarine	Stabilizes emotional blocks in throat which arise in heart feelings — purity, calmness, expression of spirit.

Table 1. Continued

Turquoise	Earth connection to sky and sea. Healing on heart, throat and navel, removes congestions on chest.
Chrysocolla	Gentle, powerful, promotes humility and listening and speaking with heart. Alleviates fears and guilts.
Amazonite	Calmness, tranquility, purifies heart of cloudy feelings and emotions.
Gold/Yellow Stones	Strengthening and Warming
Rutile Quartz	Power of the Sun, dissolves disturbances such as fear, anxiety, sadness and replaces them with strength and courage.
Golden Topaz	Inspiring and stimulating, charges heart with awareness, keenness, clarity and concentration. Balances emotional traumas.
Amber	Balances and stabilizes the heart, aids in heart ailments, strengthens.
Citrine Quartz	Wisdom and peace, aids in transmuting emotional fears, good against depression.

Table 1. Continued

Golden Fluorite	Stimulant to heart, aids in developing intuition, opens your heart toward cosmic consciousness and wisdom.
Apatite	Brings warmth and healing to sorrows or insecure feelings, emits qualities and vibrations of harmony and balance.
Gold Metal	For all stones gold is a great conductor of life energy of the Sun—all qualities of the Sun—heals sadness and depression, transmutes and perfects.
Black Stones	From Unconscious to Awareness, Grounding
Smokey Quartz	Mystical, helps to go into depths and bring to light unconscious emotional patterns, brings old pains to surface.
Black Tourmaline	Gives self-control to emotions, discipline, great staying power, clarifies abstract feelings, teaches about form.
Obsidian	Teaches that through pain and sorrow, the heart is lifted to spirit.

Table 2. Relationship of Ray, Chakra, Color and Quality

Ray & Chakra	Color	Qualities
1st	Red (primal color)	Life, strength, vitality, physical nature, courage, heat, fire, passion, outgoing.
2nd	Orange (yellow + red)	Energizes, helps to overcome anger and rage to establish self-control, essential for health and vitality, warm, stimulating, good for assimilation and circulation, regulates intake of food.
3rd	Yellow (primal color)	Symbol of mind, intellect, high intelligence, wisdom. Positive, magnetic, tonic effects on nerves — our inner sun — great equalizer for solar plexus — good for constipation.
4th	Green (yellow + blue)	Harmony, sympathy, creativity, health, abundance, nature, opens the heart. Good for compassion, giving, extending, unjudging.

Table 2. Continued

Ray & Chakra	Color	Qualities
5th	Blue (primal color)	Spiritual quest, inspiration, faith, trust, detachment, devotion, infinity, lifts, exalts. Is calm, peaceful, cooling, sedative, astringent and healing.
6th	Indigo (midnight blue with violet)	Opens 3rd eye, bridge between finite and infinite, restores long buried memories, opens door to subconscious.
7th	Violet (red + blue)	Spiritual mastery, transformation, aids in physical and psychological problems.
	White (all colors)	Purity, balance, spiritual illumination.
	Black	Form, passive, unmanifest, cosmic night, mysteries of reincarnation, seed ground of infinity.